GINGER LACEY
Fighter Pilot

The memorable story of a fantastically brave yet modest young sergeant pilot who for many years was almost unknown outside of the RAF.

Twenty-three-year-old James Henry 'Ginger' Lacey shot down an Me 109 and a Heinkel III three days after arriving in France with 501 Squadron. It was May 1940.

By the 19th June when the Squadron returned to England he had destroyed three more enemy planes, been mentioned in Despatches and awarded the Croix de Guerre.

On 12th August, the day he was awarded the DFM, he shot up two Ju 87 B; on 13th September, he destroyed the Heinkel that bombed Buckingham Palace, a success that brought him a gift of the first parachute made in Australia and a silk scarf embroidered with the names of a hundred girls employed in the factory.

By the end of September Ginger Lacey was top scorer in the Battle of Britain with eighteen enemy aircraft destroyed. To add to these were four probables and six damaged, plus five destroyed in France.

Commissioned in 1941 he became an instructor before being posted to 602 Squadron under 'Paddy' Finucane and later volunteered for rocket (airborne weapons) development. Sent overseas in 1943 he served in Burma as commanding officer of 17 Squadron. Characteristically, the then Squadron Leader shot down the first Japanese fighter he met in combat – an 'Oscar' (Nakajima Ki 43).

GINGER LACEY

Fighter Pilot

RICHARD TOWNSHEND BICKERS

UNABRIDGED

PAN BOOKS LTD · LONDON

First published 1962 by Robert Hale Ltd.
This edition published 1969 by Pan Books Ltd.,
33 Tothill Street, London, S.W.1

330 02411 6

2nd Printing 1969

*Printed & Bound in England by
Hazell Watson & Viney Ltd
Aylesbury, Bucks*

ACKNOWLEDGEMENTS

I wish to acknowledge with thanks the help given to me by the Air Ministry Air Historical Branch, which allowed me access to official records.

I also have the pleasure to acknowledge with gratitude letters of reminiscence and photographs received from the following who served under Sqdn Ldr Lacey in No. 17 Sqdn: R. H. G. Britton, D. K. Healey, P. S. Thompson, D. M. Leighton, D. A. Walde, and A. H. Witteridge (155 Sqdn).

CONTENTS

ILLUSTRATIONS

Instructor to the Yorkshire Aeroplane Club. Lacey with a joy-riding Moth, June 1939

First flying course for RAFVR pupil sergeant pilots, Perth 1937

Sergeant J. H. Lacey, September 1939

501 County of Gloucester Squadron in France, May 1940
(*Courtesy of the Imperial War Museum*)

J. H. Lacey with mother and Nicky after receiving his commission as pilot officer, January 1941
(*Courtesy of Allied Newspapers Limited, Manchester*)

Lacey on the wing of his Spitfire wearing the parachute and scarf presented by workers in the Australian parachute factory, July 1941
(*Courtesy of the Daily Sketch*)

Sqdn Ldr J. H. Lacey, P/O R. B. Connell, and P/O F. Irvine standing in front of a Spitfire, February 1945
(*Courtesy of the Imperial War Museum*)

'Jimmie Nutti', the seven-year-old Gurkha boy, found starving and ill with malaria in Calcutta and adopted by No. 17 Squadron then flying over the Burma Front
(*Courtesy of the Imperial War Museum*)

FOREWORD

by Air Chief Marshal Sir William Elliot,
GCVO, KCB, KBE, DFC

IT is perhaps characteristic of us as a nation that we are content to relegate our heroes to fiction and reluctant to recognize them in real life – and even when we do, never to call them such. Had the principal character of this book been born a Russian he would, and rightly, have been made a Hero of the Soviet Union. Instead, typically and incorrigibly, James Lacey, the Englishman from Yorkshire, will go down to posterity simply as 'Fighter Pilot', and sportingly as 'Battle of Britain Top Scorer'. I, for one, would not have it otherwise, if only because I suspect that the hero himself would recoil at the mere suggestion of the more grandiloquent version.

I met Lacey only once, fittingly on a Fighter airfield, and the impression which he made on me fits very well with the sketch which the writer has so sympathetically drawn of him. This single encounter would hardly seem to justify his request that I should write this Foreword, nor the fact that twice in our lives he was – though only indirectly and remotely owing to the difference in our ages and thus in our ranks – under my command. And so I am left to invent my own theory. Five years before he joined it, I commanded 501 Squadron. Thus I feel, and like to believe, that it may have been his thought to appoint me as his link to make his acknowledgement to that brotherhood of Officers, NCOs and men who, in the days of peace, laid the foundations of comradeship, sound training and accurate flying which later he turned to such glorious account in time of war. Two of these are mentioned as having been his companions in arms when the Squadron went to France on 10th May, 1940, Flight Lieutenant Charles Griffiths and Flying Officer A. D. Pickup, and there must have been others whose names do not actually appear in the text.

And so we come to the main theme of the book, the part which Lacey played in the Battle of Britain. In his treatment of this, the author deserves great credit. Himself an airman, he has sought to be not only the chronicler, the narrator and the biographer, but also the romanticist. Climbing into the cockpit of Lacey's Hurricane, rarely less than four and often eight times a day, he rockets us into the racing, breakneck, 300-mile-an-hour fight, twenty to thirty thousand feet above the peaceful fields of Kent and Sussex, day in day out, week after week. Here we become onlookers of a fantastic and awe-inspiring scene, that of the fiercest and most deadly form of big game hunting in the world, the fighter pilot pitted against his own kind – brave, determined and alert; cunning, stealthy and ruthless; an unerring marksman and complete master of his machine. Returning to earth, he is so weary and nerve-wracked that he immediately drops asleep under the shadow of his aircraft and vomits each time that he is woken by the Tannoy to renew his place in the terrible battle which was to prove as much for the survival of his country as of himself. He killed not with the thought of killing. 'It did not occur to him as a fight between himself and another man, but as a totally impersonal combat between two aircraft. Moreover, in his philosophy, then as now, human life was only a speck of dust in the universe and not worth worrying about greatly.'

The battle was not of the choosing of the young men who fought it, but once it was joined, they threw themselves into it with a selfless and skilful heroism which at the time drew praise from the greatest living Englishman in words which ensure that their names and deeds are immortal. For me it is a privilege to have been given the opportunity as one of the very ordinary 'many' to pay my particular tribute to one of the most extraordinary of the 'few'. And not only to him but to all and every one of the 'few'. 'Just by being airborne, reacting to each German raid, they were saving the world.' To them, on behalf of the rest of us, I address, with the kind permission of Mrs Cecil Hunt, this grace which her husband wrote and used as the chairman of the Paternosters Club during the Battle of Britain – 'For good fellowship in freedom and for those who made it possible, we give thanks.'

Stourpaine House,
Nr. Blandford, Dorset.

PREFACE

T w o achievements distinguish James Harry Lacey from other men: in the Battle of Britain he destroyed more enemy aircraft than any other pilot in Fighter Command; and one of them was the Heinkel that had bombed Buckingham Palace.

It may be argued that the latter was fortuitous, but the circumstances in which he took off on the sortie demanded a rare kind of resolution; moreover, there must be a special place in the hearts of everyone with any allegiance to or affection for the British Crown for the man who shewed the enemy that they could not with impunity attack our royal family.

Of the fact that Ginger Lacey was top scorer in a battle whose victory saved Great Britain from total defeat, there can only be one assessment: it was an immortal feat.

Despite all that has been written about The Few, Lacey's identity among them, let alone his supremacy, is little known outside the Service; perhaps because he was an NCO at the time.

When I told him that I wanted to write a book about him he characteristically replied that he doubted whether his story would interest anybody; and he had to be cajoled into this enterprise, for without his co-operation I could not have obtained the material I needed. I appreciate, and so will all those who know him, what an effort it was for him to make this contribution. I embarked on this book with a strong sense of responsibility to its subject, which soon became a realization of a peculiar privilege: it is a deeply touching experience to be entrusted by anyone with a frank revelation of his intimate emotions and experiences.

I have known Lacey for many years and we have served together both at home and abroad. The first time I heard him addressed by his wife as 'Jim' I looked round to see where the stranger was. To the Royal Air Force he is 'Ginger' Lacey, a 'character': one of our famous people, the subject of numerous legends and a person about whom we are apt to smile when his name is mentioned. I have never met anyone who disliked him; or, if they did, admitted to it – for one's sympathies would instinctively be on Ginger's side. My own feeling is that anybody who took a poor view of him would be a pretty mean sort of creature. But I know several (including myself) whom he has exasperated, infuriated and baffled: one is inclined to shake one's head in resignation about him; not as one would at a mere enfant terrible but in acceptance of an incorrigible eccentric. Being a Yorkshireman he is not effusive: he has a direct, relaxed and casual manner which is an honest expression of his indifference to what people think or are; yet he is a friendly person. He has a wide sense of humour, with a notable preference for the macabre, but a kind heart goes with it.

A man of paradox, the contradictions and surprises are everywhere: in his appearance, his attitude, his character. Essentially, he is a sensitive man who looks at life through eyes which give more warning of the ruthlessness that an outstanding fighter pilot must have than of the amiability which infuses him with such misleading calm.

Chapter One

BLOODING

T H E hand on his shoulder was rough and insistent. He rolled over, turning his back on the importunate presence, pulling the blanket tightly up to his chin, grumbling a rude dismissal; but there was an uncompromising voice, too, and reluctantly he let wakefulness seep through his mind and body.

'Three-o'clock, Sergeant ... your early call ... time to get up, Sergeant Lacey ... you're on dawn patrol ...' And there was a grubby notebook (Stationery Office issue) to sign opposite his name, as acknowledgement that he had been roused for duty; a stub of pencil, offensive with the smell of ancient, well-licked wood and blacklead, was thrust into his unwilling fingers. In the light of a torch stood a grinning airman wearing a leather jerkin buttoned over his jacket; with an air of presenting an award for virtue, he held out an enamel mug of steaming tea. 'Here you are, Sarge; thought you might like a drop of cha.'

Sergeant Pilot Lacey heaved himself on to one elbow in the shivering darkness of his tent, grunted an incoherent thanks and gulped gratefully. What an irritating war this was: for six months you flogged up and down the Bristol Channel and the English Channel giving protection to convoys that were never molested when you happened to be around, and keeping your eyes peeled for submarines which weren't there either. Then they sent the squadron to France, just when it looked as though the bitter English winter of 1939–40 was at last giving way to spring and one could even begin to think about some Easter leave. And what happened? They stuck you down on a Great War grass airfield among a lot of foreigners who wouldn't know a decent pint of bitter if it was poured down their throats from a gold tankard; they dragged you out to fly before you were decently awake; and where the hell was the enemy, anyway? Not hereabouts, for sure.

So you wriggled miserably out of your hard, rickety camp bed, wishing you were back in your own comfortable room at home in Wetherby, which was the best place in Yorkshire and therefore, for your money, in the world; or least in a snug bunk in some RAF Sergeants' Mess, like the one at Tangmere you had left only three days before. You pulled up your rough serge trousers and tottered blearily to the stream twenty yards away, where you grumblingly washed in cold water that left your fingers numb. You rubbed your chin and gave thanks that you weren't the hairy sort that couldn't decently put off shaving until you came back from patrol. You hurriedly tugged on your long, heavy sweater (the famous 'frock, white' of the RAF stores vocabulary) and your blue-chilled hands fumbled with the unpolished brass buttons of your tunic. You didn't feel passably warm until you had zipped up your fur-lined flying boots and Irvine jacket. You groped around for your flying helmet and parachute, silently fell in alongside the other two NCO pilots who were to form the dawn patrol section with you and were no more wide awake or disposed to converse than you were, and trudged to the cookhouse marquee for another mug of scalding tea.

But you had to hurry. A pale wash of light was already creeping up the sky. Presently you were walking towards the hunch-backed silhouette of your Hurricane I where your ground crew waited. You signed the Form 700 which was your official acceptance of the aircraft as fit to fly and you climbed into the cockpit.

So far everything had been routine.

The aircraft, standing unprotected all night, were cold. Lacey saw and heard the engines of his two companions start reluctantly with stabbing flames at the exhaust ports. His own refused to fire. It was a relief to have something on which to vent his annoyance at the whole tedious business of rising early to go off on yet another uneventful patrol. The starter trolley alongside was pouring electricity into the power unit; the engine turned over, the propeller spun; but the engine was too cold to fire.

He heard the wireless crackle in his headphones and his section leader asked what was the matter.

'Won't start ... of course ...' what a damned silly question.

'Catch us up if you can ... we won't wait ...'

'OK.' (This was long before the days of 'Roger' and 'Wilco', those American Army Air Corps importations.)

Morosely he watched the two Hurricanes waddle forward and go bumping out of sight over the grass. There was no control tower here to give them take-off clearance. He heard the pilots call each other.

'You OK, Red Two?'

'Yes, OK Red One.'

'Right, let's go.'

A burst of sound beat into the open canopy of his cockpit and with envy he watched them take off while he feverishly coaxed his own machine into life. They were gone in a twinkling, and then, perversely, his engine coughed, caught and roared at him to get going. He finished his checks and followed his friends.

'Knowing what I do now,' he says, 'if I'd had any sense I'd have sat on the ground and waited for them to get back.' But at the time no thought of the folly of flying alone on an offensive fighter patrol ocurred to him. Hopefully he searched for his two intended companions while climbing to 10,000 ft.

His radio was on, but it was not going to be of much use to him. The fighter squadrons of early 1940 were still equipped with single channel TR9D HF sets. These had worked admirably in England, but since 501 Squadron came to France on the 10th May, they had found that above 15,000 ft they could only receive the Overseas Programme of the BBC: a not entirely unwelcome discovery; and Lacey now looked forward to what he hoped would be a news bulletin. He wanted to know how the battle was going here in France! Instead, he was treated to popular music.

At 20,000 ft he levelled off and, since he could see nothing of the other two Hurricanes of Red Section, decided to fly towards Sedan where the Germans were reported to have broken through. It was a grand, impressive military phrase, 'broken through', and he expected to see a great deal of the smoke and moil of battle. Dawn was fine and clear. There were only a few small, widely scattered clouds beneath him. If the war was being fought down there, conditions for seeing it could not be better.

True, there was a burning village here and there, but of the enemy there was no sign. Where he had thought to see troop convoys, there were empty roads. He was at too great an altitude to discern detail, but the broad panorama of this threatened area of France on the 13th May, 1940 looked the same as any other part of the country had on any of the three days he had been flying over it.

Disappointed because it seemed that he was not going to be provided with the opportunity to report anything useful, he flew in a wide circle while he searched the sky for his two section mates. There was no sign of them.

Then, as he resignedly quartered the Sedan area and whistled under his breath to the sentimental tunes that were gently playing to him by courtesy of the BBC, an aircraft came into focus 10,000 ft below.

He was horrified to find himself suddenly staring down at a Heinkel 111 bomber. 'A big, fat Heinkel all on its own,' as he recalls with relish. But it was truly a moment of horror for him; not because he was immediately confronted with the prospect of being shot at, but because he was unexpectedly called on to exercise initiative and decision for which he had not been trained. He was a sergeant pilot and therefore not supposed to think for himself. He wanted his flight commander badly. At the least, he wanted the leadership of some experienced section leader whatever the latter's rank. At 23 years of age, despite 600 hours of flying in his log book and a year of professional instructing to his credit, a sergeant pilot who was inexperienced of combat and comparatively a novice in the Service could legitimately yearn for his flight commander.

But his flight commander wasn't there. Nobody was there, except Sergeant Lacey in his Hurricane and 10,000 ft below him the Heinkel which had not yet spotted him. For a couple of minutes he orbited, looking with curiosity at this potential victim while it cruised unconcernedly and with no sign that it was about to carry out a bombing run on some target. What should he do? Presumably he ought to attack it: but it was better not to rush these things; one didn't want to miss. Besides, this was rather a decent tune that the old BBC was putting over ... plenty of time ...

It was then that he spotted the Me 109: 5,000 ft below, halfway between him and the Heinkel; and that made him want his flight commander even more.

No. 501 Squadron had been told all about the Messerschmitt 109; in theory. None of them had seen one yet. Here was the first chance for Lacey to pick up some practical experience. And there was no hanging back to weigh it up as one could afford to do with a bomber. The Me 109 was faster than a Hurricane and had a ceiling 4,000 ft higher; it climbed better.

The official doctrine taught to fighter pilots was to open the throttle wide and attack at full speed. This was what Lacey duly did, and as he tilted into his dive he heard the BBC announcer say that Jack Teagarden and his orchestra would now play 'Oh, Johnny!'

'But,' as he says, 'the man who wrote the book hadn't done any fighting either!' His full-bore 5,000 ft descent swept him right past his target. He had a split-second's confused realization that the Me 109 was in his sights but before he could thumb the firing-button his gun-sight was blank again. So fast had he torn past that the German pilot had not even noticed him. He turned downwards, banked around and climbed for another attempt.

In the background, Jack Teagarden's boys were still dispensing 'Oh, Johnny' ...

As he positioned himself, Lacey realized that the fighter pilot's book of rules was not infallible. He had already made several psychological advances since taking off from Betheniville half an hour earlier: he had started his flight alone and when he could not find his friends had continued singlehanded; he had overcome his first discomfort at being confronted with the He 111 when there was no leader to tell him what to do; he had immediately accepted the decision he must make when he sighted the Me 109; he had attacked. And now, rattled though he had been when he saw the comparatively harmless bomber, he was able to plan his approach to the highly dangerous fighter with cool deliberation.

He adjusted his gun-sight for the wing-span of a Me 109 and for a range of 250 yards and began to stalk his victim; easing into position as though he were flying formation on the German.

And he noticed something that irritated him. His left foot was playing a tattoo on the cockpit floor. He had become conscious of this just before he committed himself to his first dive, but had forgotten about it in the effort of concentration. Now he realized that he had been flying with only his right foot on the rudder bar and his flying boot hooked into the toe-strap so as to give it purchase for applying left rudder. He glanced down and saw his foot tapping involuntarily; gave up the task of trying to control it and settled down to creeping up on the German ahead.

At 250 yards he felt quite certain that he could not hit the Messerschmitt unless he reduced the range considerably. It looked very small and far away. Opening the throttle gently he slid up to 150 yards; and still the Me 109 shewed no sign of awareness and the 'big, fat Heinkel' continued unperturbed 5,000 ft below them. It only needed one pair of sensibly watchful eyes in the bomber to catch the sun glinting on the Hurricane; and a shout of warning on the radio if they had a common frequency, or a violent agitation of the wings, would have warned the fighter. But all was as calm as a river picnic.

At 100 yards Lacey could not believe that his luck would hold much longer; yet it still seemed a long range from which to shoot. There was no point in blazing away with dashing, slap-happy optimism at any time; especially now after this protracted, careful shadowing.

At 50 yards the Me 109 filled the sights satisfactorily; it looked as big as a bus and as vulnerable: even a marksman going into action for the first time could not easily miss now.

Lacey pressed the trigger and his eight machine guns flung a storm of bullets at the narrow fuselage and the rakish wings ahead. He had scarcely time to register the flames at his gun-ports, the shuddering of his Hurricane from the guns' recoil, to sniff the cordite smoke in the cockpit or observe that the tracer ammunition looked as though solid rods were lancing from his wings to pierce the 109, when the German fighter exploded in a boiling black billow of smoke shot with red and yellow flames. There was a thunderclap of sound, a buffet from the disturbed air, he was into the enveloping smoke and out again.

Breathless with astonishment at the suddenness of this terrifying disintegration, he whipped hard round to convince himself that it really had happened. There was nothing but drifting smoke and shards of fluttering metal to shew that a Messerschmitt had ever been there.

Exhilarated, full of confidence, Lacey winged over and dived on the Heinkel. It looked an easy victim, now. The bomber had by this time, in the unpleasantest possible manner, recognized that it was not alone in the sky. It jinked hopefully, but fruitlessly, to port and starboard. It climbed sharply and dived steeply and its gunners fired a few bursts at the swooping Hurricane.

At 200 yards Lacey began shooting, closing to 20 yards, and when he pulled away he saw that one wing had been torn off the He 111 and it was spiralling steeply to the ground with a long scarf of smoke and sparks trailing behind it.

At that moment his mind registered the fact that the dance band playing in his headphones had reached the closing bars of 'Oh, Johnny!' It had not taken long to blood himself; not once but twice.

His left foot had stopped its nervous tapping. He put it back on the rudder and turned for base.

In every fighter pilot's mind there exists a vision of his first return from successful combat. A little latitude in the matter of flying regulations, perhaps: not shewing off, but a legitimate exuberance, a mild beat-up of the airfield. A victory roll. A landing to the exultant welcome of his ground crew and fellow pilots.

Lacey stepped down from his cockpit to confront mild censure. His two section mates had returned minutes before.

'What happened to you?'

'Where the hell have you been?'

'Why didn't you join up with us?'

'Why are your gun-covers blown off?'

His explanation was not well received. Nobody had reported seeing a Me 109 or a He 111 shot down that morning. Everyone knew the line-shooting type of so-and-so who would blaze away at a flock of birds and delude himself that he had taken a squirt at the foe. This sort of thing just wasn't on. Sergeant pilots who couldn't even start their engines in time to fly No. 3 in a section were not entitled to make singleton patrols and claim two scalps. One would have been indecent enough; but two! Oh, no, that sort of thing didn't wash . . .

But there was no time to sit around on the deck and natter. 'A' Flight was ordered up on another patrol: the three members of the dawn patrol section, with the other two members of the flight, one of whom was a sergeant and the other an Auxiliary Air Force flight lieutenant, Charles Griffiths, took off at once.

Once more they headed towards Sedan.

And the four sergeant pilots soon saw that their flight of five was flying a collision course with seven Me 110s. But the flight commander, who was rather older than the average fighter pilot and whose sight was not as acute as his sergeants', had failed to pick them out.

For a couple of minutes an interesting situation prevailed. Who ever said that your true fighting man itches to get at the enemy's throat whatever the cost? The truth is that your professional is as cagey as in any other walk of life: if he can get home with a whole skin he feels more satisfied than he does by being a hero. Besides, when is it meet for NCOs to draw their officer's attention to the fact that they have observed an enemy for which he is supposed, unsuccessfully, to be looking?

'We were hoping,' says Ginger Lacey, 'that he would change his course and turn away before he actually saw them.'

The Me 110 was, at that time, mistakenly reputed to be more fearsome even than the 109. Nobody was keen to dispute this.

It makes a piquant picture. The four sergeant pilots eyeing the seven enemy aircraft of which their elderly (by their standards) leader is unaware; casting wry glances at each other, exchanging the odd gesture or two: every one of them thinking 'hope he doesn't see 'em.'

And then, when the two formations are almost entangled, Charles Griffiths says: 'Let's go,' in his slow way and the five Hurricanes break furiously and in an instant there is a whirling dogfight.

Lacey picked his 110. He knew that these twin-engined fighters carried a crew of two – pilot and air gunner – with five machine guns and two cannons. They were faster than a Hurricane and had an all-round field of fire for both defence and attack.

The Me 110 dived and Lacey, his left foot thudding the floor and his right hooked into the starboard rudder pedal, followed it. Tracer licked up at him and he instinctively ducked as he saw it flick overhead. He was close enough to fire a burst himself and he saw the orange splashes of strikes along the enemy's fuselage: he was more confident of his accuracy than he had been a short two hours ago. The Messerschmitt stall-turned. Lacey took a quick glance in his mirror to see that there was nobody on his tail and turned after it. It banked sharply to port and he banked inside it; at the instant that it levelled off he got in a two-second burst that raked the wings and the port engine cowling. So far, the 110 had not lived up to its name. Lacey was beginning to enjoy himself; a momentary vision of the two hostiles he had destroyed that morning cheered and encouraged him: but this was proving to be a longer flight than both the others and he felt sweat on his neck and chest from mental and physical exertion.

Another near miss made him kick hard out of the way: the tracer almost scraped the Hurricane's belly. And still they were going down. From dead astern and above he put a burst into the port engine; and then the fire started: he saw flames from the dead engine flung by the wind towards the Me's cockpit canopy. One more careful burst and the whole wing was alight and the aircraft began turning slowly on to its back; but still the gunner was shooting at the Hurricane. With a sharp flick the 110 completed its half roll and went into a twisting vertical dive. Lacey went down to make sure that it did not recover. He saw it crash in a field and watched briefly while French troops ran out from a wood towards the wreckage.

Staring upward as he climbed at full throttle, he could see a skein of aircraft darting about in an undefined pattern at about 20,000 ft. The fight was still on, it seemed; his place was up there in it, not down here verifying the destruction of an obviously uncontrollable victim.

He wriggled uncomfortably on his parachute: it felt as though he had been on this seat for hours; he eased his collar away from his neck and brushed sweat from his face with the back of his gloved hand.

They were still there, the silhouettes above him; still apparently weaving and feinting. Damn this altimeter! Only 15,000 ft yet. Would it never get to 20,000?

At 18,000 ft, his eyes screwed half-shut against the glare, he felt as though he had walked around a blind, dark corner straight into a mule's kick. His stomach contracted and while he still looked up and over his shoulder at the Me 110s, 2,000 ft above, he was putting his aircraft into a steep dive. That was no dogfight he had been in such a hurry to join: it was the surviving Messerschmitts flying nose to tail in a defensive circle; and there wasn't another British fighter in sight.

The German pilots had recognized the Hurricane at the same moment that Lacey appreciated his danger. Here was an easy prize in the worst possible position: down sun and climbing slowly. They broke and pounced together.

Diving vertically from 18,000 ft Lacey watched the German fighters in his mirror: tearing down with two 1,150 hp engines propelling their seven-ton weight, they were measurably overhauling the three-ton Hurricane with its single 1,030 hp power unit. He could see them looming nearer as the landscape hurtled up to meet him. If he had sweated before, it was a mild reaction compared with what he was exuding now.

It was an effort to keep his head back and watch the mirror, against the tremendous force of 'g' that hammered at him. His aircraft was vibrating and whining with speed and he pushed the stick further forward to coax the last degree of perpendicularity and the last yard of speed from the protesting airframe.

With his ears pounding he suddenly felt control snatched away from him.

It was as though the world had collapsed, imprisoning him in a cocoon where violent forces heaved and tore at him simultaneously from all directions. A hideous sensation ripping and clawing at his body, his mind in darkening confusion, he had a semi-conscious knowledge that the Hurricane had dragged itself away from the control of his hands on the stick and his feet on the rudder bar and was flying itself.

It had bunted right over the perpendicular and done an outside loop onto its back. But it had saved him: the crazy, involuntary manoeuvre had swept him right out of his pursuers' ken. None of the Messerschmitt pilots cared to emulate this aerobatic! Lacey would not have attempted it himself, in the most frantic efforts to evade them; but it had happened, and as he regained his clear-headedness to find that the fighter was straight and level, though inverted, he rolled dazedly out and found himself alone in the sky.

An aircraft less sturdy than the Hurricane could not have survived without having its wings ripped off. The loading on them was so heavy that the perspex covers over the landing lights were sprung out of position. And in the manoeuvre, although he did not know the name for it then, its pilot had experienced compressibility for the first time.

Shaken but thankful, he saw Rheims come into view. 501 Squadron's base at Betheniville was near the city. Sourly he asked himself what sort of a disbelieving reception he could expect this time. But at least he had not been alone, the others had seen him go after a Me 110 and his claim to have destroyed it should not fall on such sceptical ears as before.

But there was marked cordiality awaiting him: a French anti-aircraft gun site had telephoned to report that a Hurricane had shot down a Me 109 and a He 111 near Sedan that morning.

Sergeant Lacey had fought his first air battle and his second in the space of a few hours. He had blooded himself threefold.

He was destined to multiply his kills tenfold before, 1,500 flying hours and five years later, he fired his guns in action for the last time, in his 87th combat, as a squadron commander over Burma.

He had a lot to think about and the Intelligence Officer was importuning him for a combat report; but for the time being he had no desire for anything but breakfast.

Chapter Two

BEGINNINGS

Y O U are a prosperous, cautious Yorkshire cattle dealer; not opposed unreasonably to innovation, but inclined to be reactionary. Your son pipes up one morning at breakfast and says he'd like to join the Royal Air Force. You look at him with approval and an indulgent smile: it's a very natural expression for a twelve-year-old; a couple of years ago it was engine driver, and before and since that there have been phases of yearning to be a deep sea diver, a bus conductor (because of the machine with the engaging little bell), a detective and a cowboy. Now it is an air pilot. You pat the little lad on the head and go your way with a mildly amusing yarn to tell your pals over a pint next market day.

Two years later, young Jim mentions again, pointedly, that a Halton apprenticeship can lead to a pilot's cockpit. You are still benevolent about his obsession. It shews the lad's growing up: at least he hasn't changed his mind about his career for a long time. You attribute the ambition largely to the attraction of wearing a uniform: King James's Grammar School at Knaresborough has a pretty efficient Boy Scout troop and your youngster is one of its keenest members. True, it's not all uniform and badges with him: he enjoys the comradeship and the camping, the wide games, the pioneering of scouting. Moreover, the RAF is getting a lot of publicity these days: it's 1931 and every Englishman is proud and excited about the Schneider Trophy, which a RAF team has just won for Britain. Everybody is becoming air-minded in this decade; you don't deny that: and it's not only the Service that is blazing the way. Look at Amy Johnson, for instance; aye, a Yorkshire lass. Of course. But 'What's that, Jim? You want to join the RAF? Aye, you do that, son.' You chuckle and go on your way: there's real work to be done in the cattle trade and you can't hang about at home listening to a boy's day dream, fond though you are of him.

But when, at the age of sixteen, Jim Lacey told his father with conviction that he wanted to enter the RAF Apprentices' School at Halton, the latter realized that they had reached a crisis which had to be reckoned with. There was a firmness of purpose about the boy that called for serious man-to-man treatment. He was a quiet chap, and not given to making a fuss either when he was dejected or elated; but if he made up his mind to achieve something you couldn't put him off without a cogent reason.

What were the arguments for and against? Well, they were all against; summed up, it came to just this: the RAF was a short way to suicide. It was no use pointing out that aeroplanes were becoming safer every day; that they were being flown to Australia by young women; to India by rich playboys; that a one-eyed American Indian could pilot one safely to distant places. They were still nasty, dangerous things to the generation that had grown up with a wary eye even on motor cars. If you were fond of your son and believed it your duty to protect him from danger and ensure him a life-span of decent length, you could not agree to his embracing so perilous an occupation. That was final. And on the credit side, you offered this: 'When you leave school, go to an agricultural college and I'll take a farm for you.' What could be fairer than that?

To a boy brought up in a conventional pre-war home, with a proper respect for his parents and a genuine affection for them, this was bound to seem a fair and acceptable proposition. One didn't upset one's mother and father by stubborn wilfulness.

So Jim Lacey, albeit reluctantly, put aside his own wishes and acceded to his father's.

'But,' he says, 'just before I was due to leave school I suddenly realized for the first time that being a farmer was a life sentence! It's a seven day a week job, twenty-four hours a day. When the farm needs you, you've got to be there.'

And there speaks the Ginger Lacey who is familiar to so many: something of a lotus-eater by instinct, not perhaps the most industrious of mortals, born in another clime and of a different colour he would likely have been content to recline on a warm beach (in the shade) and open his mouth occasionally to let some succulent fruit drop into it. It would not, however, be fair to construe his distaste for farming as a mere unwillingness to sacrifice his freedom. We see here also an honest reluctance to tackle anything which he knows he is not going to have the will to carry out thoroughly. An indolent man doesn't survive 87 combats as a fighter pilot; even the briskest man doesn't live through that amount of fighting unless he has put in a lot of hard work learning to be a master of his calling.

So, this decision made, what was he to do instead? He had passed his School Certificate with credits: among them, chemistry and botany. He enjoyed chemistry: he would, then, exploit his talent and satisfy his liking by becoming a chemist. He apprenticed himself as a student pharmacist.

'It is just as well,' he recalls soberly, 'that I didn't go into farming. In 1933, the year that I left school, farming was at the rock bottom of its slump.' It was in this year, also, that his father died. Sadly, he helped his mother to sell off their stock at the low prices then prevailing and went on with his pharmaceutical studies. For the latter he really did not have much heart: the denial of a RAF career had been a more grievous blow to him than he had shewn; and he had been mistaken in his assumption that working in a chemist's shop meant 'doing chemistry' as he had done it in the school laboratories. It was, he discovered, mainly a matter of selling perfumes and bath salts, of wrapping up tins of cough lozenges and bottles of linctus in neat, white paper parcels sealed with a blob of red wax, of dispensing single razor blades to stubbly-chinned old men who looked as though they made them last from one month to the next. He had gone into pharmacy not because he really wanted to but because he wasn't allowed to go into the air force: his father had put his foot down. So there he was, the most undedicated young student pharmacist in Yorkshire; and it was the disillusion about 'doing chemistry' that had spoiled for him something that he might in time have been able to accept; perhaps even with enthusiasm.

It was a three-year apprenticeship. Three years of pausing in the act of taking a bottle from the shelf or a box from the counter, arrested by the sound of an aeroplane flying overhead. Three years of reading enviously in the newspapers about the fun and achievements of others: there were air displays and exploratory flights and flights that broke records for altitude, endurance or distance. Three years that dragged by with aching slowness, filled inadequately by poring over books on aviation, talking about aeroplanes with your air-minded friends, and even listening with absorption to the maudlin reminiscences of a regular customer for corn plasters who wore a faded, soup-stained and frayed RFC tie with defiant panache. Even though one knew he had been nothing more belligerent than an Air Mechanic, there was a breath of adventure and freedom in his hoarse allusions to Ball and Mannock, Sopwith Camels and BE2s.

The three years between sixteen and nineteen, between boyhood and manhood, are the slowest and longest in life. But at last, Jim Lacey's bondage ended. He took his intermediate examinations and turned his back on pharmacy for ever. Standing on the pavement, with the shop door shut for the last time behind him, he paused for a moment to breathe the keen autumn air and savour the freedom that was his after a seeming eternity of being fettered by a humdrum indoor job. He heard a familiar drone overhead and looked up. Moving across the darkening sky, a pair of bright lights — one red, the other green — brightly symbolized the far horizons that beckoned to him so strongly.

A passer-by, hurrying along with his head bent in a townsman's stoop and his shoulders hunched against the cold, butted into him; hardly raising his head, the man grumbled and pottered on. Young Lacey felt sorry for him. Poor devil, with his gaze fixed half a yard beyond the toecaps of his boots: what would he ever see but the grime of the pavement and dirty rainwater in the gutters? Lacey kept his eyes on the twinkling navigation lights five thousand feet above and watched them until they were gone and the single yellow light in the aircraft's tail gleamed no more strongly than a pinprick in the heavens.

'So,' he says, with West Riding prosaicness, 'I joined the RAF Volunteer Reserve.' His mother treated his decision with good sense. It was his life, she felt, to live or to end as he wished. Lacey adds, with fond irony, 'She didn't really think I'd be accepted by the Medical Board anyway when she gave me permission to go and have my medical.'

'When she gave me permission to go and have my medical.' A simple phrase, which reveals more of the speaker's upbringing and character than a page of other people's opinions about him. At nineteen, the youth with adventure in his blood who had left school three years ago and worked at a man's job, still asked his mother's leave to join the RAFVR.

Two of his friends in the rugger club – strapping front row forwards – had preceded him and both were turned down. Who would suppose that the rather pale wing three-quarter of scarcely middle stature who did not look impressively robust would pass?

But he did. There was an interview and he passed that too. And now, for the first time, doubt set in. Never a garrulous sort, he kept his enrolment a secret even from his brother. His mother was the only one who knew that he was going to try to learn to fly. It would be time enough to mention it to others when he had succeeded; better to say nothing at all now, in case he should fail: it would be bitter enough to support such disappointment without having to bear the inevitable jibes that must accompany it.

Thirty embryo sergeant pilots – the first course of them in the VR – assembled at Scone, in Scotland. No. 740042 Lacey, J. H., C of E, born Wetherby 1st February 1917, was one of them. He was also the first to fly solo: in 6 hours 55 minutes, in a Tiger Moth; which was good, particularly for the RAF, which errs if anything on the side of caution.

Flight Lieutenant Nick Lawson was his instructor. 'A nicer chap you could never find. A born instructor. If I ever did become anything respectable in the way of a pilot, it was certainly due to Nick Lawson and not because I had any inborn ability.' Nevertheless, Lacey admits that he took naturally to flying.

At the end of the course he was assessed 'Above Average'

and has maintained at least this grading throughout his flying career; there are several endorsements in his log books which award him 'Exceptional'.

What does a young man who has wanted to fly since he was a schoolboy and who is destined to become an outstandingly able pilot feel the first time that he is airborne?

Lacey had been looking forward to this moment for eight years, more keenly than he had ever anticipated any event. He thought he could foretell the sensations and emotions that were in store for him: after all, books and films had painted vivid, realistic pictures. The actuality exceeded expectations as all empirical emotion must surpass the vicarious.

Within four hours of arriving at Scone airfield, he was strapped into the rear cockpit of a Tiger Moth a thousand feet above the Perthshire hills. His eyes darted from the gently jiggling joystick to the rudder bar which moved a few inches this way and that as Nick Lawson turned; from the airspeed indicator impressively shewing 70 mph to the altimeter which was climbing through the hundreds into its second thousand; from the purple hills to the dark green valleys; from the miniature houses, vehicles and farm animals beneath to the canvas and wire of the wings that hummed a few feet away from him.

Through the Gosport tube came the instructor's voice, telling him to touch the controls gently and follow their movements. Eagerly he put his hand on the stick and his feet on the rudder bar and tried to imagine that the helmeted head in front was not there; that he was alone up here with the sun-drenched wisps of cloud, the majestic mountain tops and the hovering eagle. A gruff command told him not to hold so damned tight and to put less pressure on the rudder controls with his clumsy feet. He didn't mind. He didn't mind what anybody said to him, as long as he could stay here and enjoy this superb elation, this stupendous release that was as much spiritual as physical. The one worry he had now was that he might not be efficient at his task: to cease flying training was the only tragedy of magnitude that he could envisage. He relaxed, cupping his fingers gently around the stick and letting his shoes rest lightly on the bar. 'That's better,' said Lawson.

'I wonder if he'll think I'm cocky if I ask him to do a loop,' thought his pupil.

It was gratifying to be sent solo before his companions. It was not until he was at five hundred feet and circling the aerodrome that he wondered if he would ever be able to get down again: he had a momentary vision of himself as an aerial Flying Dutchman, destined to orbit Scone in a Tiger Moth until the Last Trump; then he remembered that Tiger Moths only stayed airborne while there was petrol in their tanks and if he wanted to put this one back on the ground without bending it he had better fix his mind on reality.

Learning to fly in Scotland was appropriate, for his mother came from Caithness. Her father, Captain James Smith, had been a Master Mariner; and perhaps there could be no better heritage than Jim Lacey's for a man born to fight in the fiercest aerial battle in history: on the one side, the adventurous spirit of the seafarer and on the other the conservative rationalism of a father who made his living among farmers. Maybe, indeed, it was the worthiness of both his Scottish and Yorkshire forebears rather than the streak of sailor's daring that contributed more to his will to beat the enemy.

His 65 hours of flying at Scone, half of them solo, were accomplished in six weeks and he returned home to continue flying at Brough during weekends. Here he flew the Blackburn B2, a side-by-side two seater of about the same dimensions and weight as the Tiger Moth.

Proudly, his mother told their friends and relations that Jim was now a qualified pilot; and he found it pleasing to acknowledge this casually. It had been worthwhile to keep his aspirations to himself. The savour of admiration and envy, after success, was sweet and rich.

He found a new comradeship among his flying companions. The first sensations associated with flying are the smells of fabric dope, oil, petrol, hot metal and rubber mountings that cling to airfields and aircraft the world over. The first time anyone enters an aeroplane, this is the impression that immediately registers: here is a pursuit with its own special odours, like those of hay and manure in a stable or damp jerseys and muddy boots in a changing room. People who fly react to this aura of their mystique as others do to the aroma of good whisky or the scent of a rose garden. And, bound together in the sodality of mutual understanding, they have a particular kind of common bond also: flying, fundamentally, is something at which you take the risk (however mild this may be rendered by rigid safety precautions) of hurting or killing yourself; therefore people who indulge in it have an unconscious respect for each other. Out of this emerges a spirit of friendship which can only prevail when danger is not very far in the background. In a few weeks he knew his flying friends better than he did those with whom he had been at school or played rugger.

There was no need to think about a humdrum job any longer. The RAFVR paid a good training allowance, and with regular attendance at weekends, this was adequate pocket money. Now and again, when he felt like spending a little extra, he would help out in somebody's business from Monday to Friday. But whatever his hands were doing, his mind and heart were fixed on Saturday morning when he could catch the bus to Brough.

When he had put in 60 hours on Blackburn B2s, the Training School received its first Hawker Harts.

Here was an aeroplane to bring a gleam to the eye. More than twice the weight of the other two types which Lacey had flown, it had a maximum speed of 184 mph, compared with their 110. Its length and span were impressively greater and it had a ceiling of over 21,000 ft; he had not yet been above 10,000 ft, a height to which the Hart could climb in eight minutes.

There were only two pilots at the school with enough flying time behind them to be capable of flying this paragon, and Lacey was one of them. Now, on Saturdays and Sundays, he was told to go off on his own and put in as many hours as he could; he usually entered another eight in his log book before returning home.

Before 1938 was over, he underwent an instructors' course at Grimsby, passed the examination of the Guild of Air Pilots and Navigators, and obtained an instructor's endorsement on his licence.

This was the decisive point in his life, more significant than his abandonment of pharmacy or his enrolment in the RAFVR; the course on which he determined now gave him the experience and skill to survive the severe tests and perils of the future.

His mother, watching him across the supper table that first night back from Grimsby, recognized the signs of preoccupation in his face. His brother Charles, now a medical student, later to be a RAMC parachutist doctor and fated to die at 29, noticed it too.

'What's biting you, Jim?'

'I was thinking.'

'Hang on to that thought; it's likely to be lonely!'

But Jim wasn't rising to any bait this evening.

'What are you thinking about, son?'

'Flying, mother.'

'I know that. But what about flying, this time?'

'It's the only life for me, you know. I don't mean just this weekend stuff: that's champion fun, of course; but I want to do more than that.'

'I see. What have you got in mind?'

'Well, now that I've got my instructor's ticket, I think I'll try for a job with the Yorkshire Aeroplane Club.'

Charles said what was in all their minds. 'You're not thinking, lad: you've decided.'

His brother grinned, looking uncertainly across at their mother.

'Well,' she asked briskly, 'I suppose you'll be applying for this job tomorrow?'

The Secretary of the Yorkshire Aeroplane Club was patient and polite. She was accustomed to handling nervous members, even to coping with boisterous ones who celebrated a first solo too bibulously. But a slightly mad juvenile was a new and unsettling phenomenon.

She eyed the rather short, slim, fair-skinned youth who sat in her visitors' chair, and made yet another attempt to understand; and to persuade him to understand, which was more important.

'So you want to join the club?'

'In a way, yes.'

'To learn to fly.' She did not put it as a question, this time: she tried to state it firmly as a fact, the logical and only reason for wishing to join a flying club; but, to her annoyance, she heard her voice falter as she faced that level, candid and half-amused stare. Inconsequentially a small voice at the back of her mind reminded her that if ever she had seen real flyer's eyes she was looking into them now: pale grey-blue and sharp. Putting the distracting thought aside with mild annoyance she braced herself for the answer. If this exasperatingly persistent, apparently obtuse, and presumably runaway schoolboy repeated his absurdity about wanting to instruct, she felt she would have to scream.

'No,' he said, 'I want to be an instructor.'

Hold it, she told herself, *this is what you're paid for: to put up with imbeciles, and kids who would have stowed away on a sailing ship, for adventure, in the last generation.* 'Yes. Yes, of course. You want to instruct. Quite. But before you can do that you'll have to learn to fly yourself, won't you?'

'But I *can* fly ...'

'How old are you? Sixteen ... seventeen? When have you had time to learn to fly?'

'I'm twenty-one,' said Lacey, politely putting his logbook on the table.

The secretary went so pale that she looked almost the same colour as her tormentor. She glanced at the first page of the log book. Flicked over about a dozen sheets. Muttered 'two hundred and fifty hours' under her breath, crossly, scrutinized his licence, and reached for the telephone. 'Give me the Chief Flying Instructor,' she said, not taking her eyes off her visitor with the deprecating manner.

What's up with her? Lacey was thinking, *Surely I can't have annoyed her? If I did ... oh, sister! Wait until I really try to be irritating.*

Unexpectedly he smiled at her and she smiled back unthinking. 'As a matter of fact, we have got a vacancy for another instructor ...'

The next twelve months were halcyon ones. Today he might

be instructing, tomorrow flying by day or night around the Territorial Army gun sites to give the soldiers aiming practice; the next day, he might fly a club member down to London for a few hours' business, the day after give joy-rides to cash customers at five shilling for ten minutes. 'Flying at its best,' he calls it, 'none of this bus-driving like an airline pilot has to do. Just the kind of flying I like.'

Even his annual holiday was spent flying, on annual attachment to a regular RAF squadron for training.

On completing 250 hours' flying, Volunteer Reserve pilots were invited to carry out these periods of duty by a letter from the Air Ministry. Young Lacey was delighted to see that the signatory was a group captain who courteously claimed to be 'Your obedient Servant'. Being, as he says, 'very much a civilian', he acknowledged the invitation with a gracious indication that he would be prepared to accept it provided that he went to a squadron flying single-seater fighters on the south coast. In order to make the group captain's task easier, he went so far as to express a preference for No. 1 Squadron, at Tangmere (Sussex), which was equipped with Furies.

Whether it was resignation which prompted the group captain, or kindness of heart or some innate sense warning him (as was to dawn on many others in the future) that he had encountered simultaneously an immovable obstacle and an irresistible force, is not known; but one afternoon in late January 1939 saw Sergeant Lacey arrive at Tangmere for six weeks' attachment.

The Hawker Fury was slightly smaller than the two-seat Hart. Its wing span was over 7 ft less, its fuselage about 3 ft shorter and it had a loaded weight some 500 lb lighter. Moreover, its top speed was 240 mph.

For three weeks, the laconic Volunteer Reserve sergeant pilot from Yorkshire revelled in the high speed and manoeuvrability of this fighter; in the formation flying that called on every ounce of his skill and experience; in shooting at a towed drogue. It was the last that gave rise to most comment among the regulars. Sergeant Lacey's flying ability was high enough to win mild praise: nobody expected much of a mere amateur weekend flyer and he was, after all, a professional pilot in civilian life. But his marksmanship was far above average and was partly explained by the quickness with which he picked out other aircraft when a formation went up on battle practice. His outstandingly good eyesight was responsible for both the first warning that 'hostile' aircraft were approaching and for the extraordinary number of hits he could score on an air-gunnery target.

Early one morning at the beginning of his fourth week of attachment, he stood on the tarmac outside the squadron hangar, with the other pilots, watching the arrival of a hump-backed monoplane fighter in the circuit. Before it had landed, three more were overheard and presently sixteen of these monsters were lined up at the edge of the airfield. The ferry pilots who had brought them paused only long enough to drink a cup of NAAFI tea, smoke a cigarette to take the taste away, and climb into the Furies. Feeling like small boys being deprived of a cherished toy, No. 1 Squadron watched their Hawker Furies disappear and walked over to take stock of their Hawker Hurricanes.

Poking its nose 13 ft 3 in into the air, 3 ft higher than the little Fury, with a wing span 10 ft greater, a fuselage 5 ft longer, and a weight of 6,000 lb compared with its predecessor's 3,600 lb, the Hurricane was a daunting sight.

Lacey walked round one, in silence, with a senior regular flight sergeant. When they had completed their external inspection, the latter pushed his forage cap to the back of his head and looked disgusted and awed. 'Blimey. A single-seat troop carrier!'

Lacey said, quite simply, that he did not feel that he would ever be able to fly one. Sergeant 'Lofty' Luckham, however, who had qualified on these strange beasts, soon dispelled this lack of confidence with some encouraging words. As a briefing, his introduction of Lacey to the Hurricane was admirably succinct. 'Don't touch that lever in the right hand corner of the cockpit there, while you're on the ground, or the aeroplane will fall down. Otherwise, she's exactly the same as a Fury.'

'If you say so.' The Volunteer Reserve sergeant looked at the regular, detected no trace of a leg-pull, hoisted himself into the cockpit and took off. 'I didn't touch the lever in the right hand corner, while on the ground; or in the air: nor, I must admit, did I touch it for the next two flights either: I had no confidence whatsoever in retractable undercarriages at that time and wasn't sure that the wheels would ever come down again.'

He was in no hurry to return to the Yorkshire Aeroplane Club and resume his civilian occupation. Indeed, his visit to Tangmere had come at an opportune time: just previously, he had 'written off' an aircraft belonging to his employers through, he admits 'to a certain extent, my own fault.'

The Tipsy 'B' was a delightful little light two-seat monoplane with a 60 hp engine: even the Blackburn B2 had a 120 hp motor. In theory, it was impossible to spin this aircraft. Lacey disproved this; albeit unwittingly.

Having spent an hour over the aerodrome, trying unsuccessfully to spin the Tipsy 'B', he turned to his passenger, shrugged and said, 'Well, we'd better go in to land.'

The passenger, who had reacted with mixed feelings to their inability to spin, nodded agreeably. Honour was satisfied and spinning is a stomach-churning sensation. Besides, who was to know that would happen if the unspinnable aeroplane was forced to spin? It would probably prove to be unrecoverable too, once compelled into an unnatural function.

A moment later he found out, as Lacey throttled back on the approach.

With only three hundred feet of air beneath them, and well inside the aerodrome perimeter, Lacey felt the aircraft lurch into a spin, taking him by surprise.

He had barely time to tell himself that the makers' claim was not entirely justifiable after all, and even mildly congratulate himself on succeeding (even accidentally) where others had failed, when the little aeroplane plunged nose first into the middle of the grass airfield.

With a rending of canvas and cracking of wood, it ploughed along the ground bucking and twisting. The engine roared deafeningly. Lacey saw his passenger's mouth open in a cry of alarm, but the sound was muted by the terrifying noises of the crash. For a few seconds he was filled with fear and horror; and with anger at himself for endangering his passenger through an error. But the violence of sound and motion ended in sudden, complete silence as he cut the ignition and the petrol feed. Flung about in their straps one moment, pilot and passenger found themselves an instant later at rest and dazedly undoing the buckles.

Scrambling out of the tangle of splintered wood and torn fabric, they saw a fleet of cars racing out of the car park near the club house. Not far behind them ran the club steward, his white coat gleaming in the sun. He appeared to be carrying a tray.

Lacey nodded to his passenger. 'You all right?'

'Fine. And you?'

'I'm OK. But I could do with a drink.'

'Looks as though the steward thought of that.'

They watched the cars sink gradually into the soft ground on the outskirts of the field. Presently the rescuers were churning slowly through mud, in bottom gear; and the steward, his legs going like a Derby winner's, had overtaken them.

Within three minutes of the accident, he arrived, red faced and out of breath; a tray in his hands and on the tray two balloon glasses.

'I brought you two double brandies, sir.' He stood there, deferential and panting.

Lacey gestured politely to his companion. 'After you.'

'No thanks: I don't drink.'

'Don't you, by George? Well I do!' And Lacey obligingly drank them both. Then, inspecting the wreckage with the insouciance of one who has survived many such misfortunes, he remarked, 'H'm. That elevator's quite unharmed. As good as new. All they need do is wheel another fuselage and wings under it and they've got a perfectly good aeroplane.'

A senior club official, having flogged his car in bottom gear across several hundred yards of bumpy, boggy ground, to rescue a presumably badly injured instructor and member, was not pleased to overhear this.

'While the Directors forgot about my little effort there, I went down and did six weeks with 1 Squadron,' explains Lacey, looking back.

When he returned to Yorkshire, his misdemeanour had been

swamped by much graver events. Germany was spoiling for trouble; and this time it looked as though she was going to find it.

All the instructors at the Club were on one or other of the RAF reserves and imminently expecting to be called up. Ginger Lacey, with the recent memory of squadron bandinage, endless 'shop' over pints of beer in Sussex pubs, and flying a Hurricane at 300 mph, was not reluctant to return to regular Service life. Despite his natural independence and his relish for civilian freedom, he had quickly acquired a taste for RAF customs and the unobtrusive esprit de corps which infuses every squadron. He did not know it, but he was rapidly approaching the threshold of what was to become a permanent career.

Chapter Three

THE BALLOON GOES UP

T H E closer danger looms the calmer the British become. When it arrives, they acknowledge it with some under-stated phrase. The 3rd September 1939 was recognized as 'the day on which the balloon went up'. This was as happy a description as could have become cliché, for it had a literal connotation also: the bloated silver barrage balloons which floated up on their cables around every major military target in the British Isles.

Sergeant Lacey was ordered to report on Saturday, 2nd September, to his Town Centre in Hull. He heard the Prime Minister's broadcast telling the nation it was at war with Germany, at the bar of the Hedon Aero Club on 3rd September, with a pint of bitter in his hand and in company with a score or more of other called-up reserve pilots. A lot of alcohol had flowed almost unceasingly since the previous day: another British habit when confronted with patriotic obligations of the more violent order.

'It didn't mean a lot to me, but the prospect of fighting in a war scared me stiff.' He was not alone.

The only practical worry he had was about his posting. He hoped it would be to a squadron which was equipped with Hurricanes and stationed in some pleasant place. After having put in about thirty hours on Hurricanes, he did not want to return to biplanes; and there were a few Gladiator squadrons still. Nor did he want to find himself on some remote station where the only amusement would be to drink in the Sergeants' Mess: he wanted to have a choice in where he did his drinking of an evening. He might even want to go to a cinema or do some shopping.

Things could have been worse: he was sent to 501 (County of Gloucester) Squadron, an Auxiliary Air Force unit, which was based at Filton, a suburb of Bristol. Like all RAFVRs he looked darkly on the AAF which, in peacetime, had only officer pilots and was regarded by VRs as a rather snobbish preserve of the rich. In order to make the auxiliary squadrons up to their wartime establishment, NCO pilots were posted to them from the reserve.

501 Squadron, which had been given Hurricanes only a few days before the declaration of war, found itself with a lot of commissioned pilots who had never flown them and several strange reserve sergeants who had. The squadron owned a Fairey Battle equipped for dual flying and it was decreed that, as a face-saving measure for the officers, no NCO pilot would be allowed to handle a Hurricane until he had checked out on this. The officers were all automatically considered proficient to fly Hurricanes as they had each at some time, flown the Battle; and none of the sergeants had enjoyed this privilege! By this unsubtle compromise, the officers were given time to break themselves in to a new machine while the NCOs wasted their time and the taxpayers' money as well as petrol, on a retrogressive schedule. However, within a month the whole squadron was operational.

Operations, for the time being, consisted of convoy patrols over the Bristol Channel: looking not only for enemy aircraft but for submarines. 'We were seeing submarines, too. There weren't any there; but we were seeing them.' An astonishing number of different types of disturbance on the water can be mistaken for the ripple of a periscope, when flying at five thousand feet or even lower. Everyone was bursting with enthusiasm for the real war to break out and it was to be expected that frequent false identifications should be reported.

The convoy patrols were flown during the day, and after dark there was night flying practice. Lacey soon put himself in the dog-house.

The Squadron Adjutant, a regular officer, was a Qualified Flying Instructor from the Central Flying School. On the first evening that Sergeant Lacey was detailed for night flying, the Adjutant had a short conversation with him.

'How much Service night flying have you done, Sergeant?'

'None, sir.'

Standing there innocently in the locker room, with his Irvine jacket half open and his young, guileless face giving no hint of what was going on in his mind, Lacey was a born con. man; but the Adjutant had no way of knowing this. Yet. Nor would Lacey have admitted that he was leading the QFI up the garden path. He had been asked a definite question, to which he had given a truthful answer.

'Well,' said the Adjutant and Flying Instructor briskly, 'I'd better give you a spot of dual in the Hart trainer.'

Lacey courteously acknowledged the good sense of this suggestion. The QFI glowed with inward satisfaction and pleasure. Some of these non-regulars were a bit rough and bolshie: made a change when you ran across a decent, amenable youngster like this one. The Adjutant was all of twenty-six himself.

Together they walked out to the trainer, the Adjutant making friendly comments on the suitability of the weather for a night exercise and the prospects of someone seeing a genuine U-boat in the near future for a change. Sergeant Lacey kept his thoughts to himself.

Full of bonhomie, confident that it wouldn't take long to familiarize this quite experienced reservist with night flying technique, the Adjutant demonstrated a couple of circuits and landings. Then, 'You have control, Sergeant Lacey. Try a landing.' Amiable, that's what he was; downright amiable and he was striding straight into a pitfall if only he did but know.

'Very good, sir.' Lacey was downright respectful; which, had the Adjutant known his sergeant, would have been a red light to him.

Lacey began his approach. A little high, he felt. An instant later, a startled QFI found himself clutching the rim of his cockpit for support as he was thrown steeply to one side. Sergeant Lacey was side-slipping off his excess height. They touched down gently and the Adjutant burst into wrathful life.

'What the hell do you mean by doing side-slips at night, Sergeant? Here it is, your first attempt at night flying, and you behave like a barn-storming circus pilot. You've got no common sense, man. Slide-slipping on your first night flight! I never heard anything like it. I've a good mind to put you on a charge.'

'But I always side-slip off extra height, sir.'

'Not at night, you fool.'

'Yes, sir; at night, sir. Always, sir.'

'But ... but you told me you hadn't done any night flying, Sergeant.'

'No sir. You asked me if I had any *Service* night flying, and I quite honestly told you I hadn't. Actually, I've got over a hundred hours' night flying on civil aircraft.'

Unfortunately, a hundred hours of night flying was considerably more than the Adjutant could claim for himself.

Lacey says, 'After that I was allowed to go off at night in a Hurricane. *And* side-slip it if I felt like it.'

That sort of thing is all right if you can get away with it; and, if you are a good enough performer, you will get away with it: but pilots who attempt feats which will demonstrate their skill – and the night flying incident was not calculated showing off, but an instinctive reaction to a familiar situation – too often exceed their ability.

There was a sergeant pilot on 263 Squadron, which was also at Filton, who provided a talking point at about this time.

No. 263 had converted from Gladiators to Spitfires before this pilot joined them. He had already flown the latter, but never the former. Then the squadron was chosen for the campaign in Norway and its Spitfires were replaced by Gladiators. The sergeant, making his first flight in one of the latter, decided to repeat a familiar practice of all the Filton pilots: flying under the railway bridge across the Severn. There was nothing particularly hazardous about this, for there was ample clearance. The sergeant pilot, who was used to the slim monoplane Spitfire with its retractable undercarriage, habitually went within inches of the river's surface. The Gladiator was not only a biplane, it had a fixed undercarriage. The pilot, allowing too much clearance for the overhead wing, also misjudged his height above the river and gouged the surface. This pulled the aircraft onto its nose. The propeller flailed the yellow water into boiling foam and dragged the aeroplane under. Nearly a minute later, vomiting with shock, pain and hastily swallowed muddy water, the pilot floated up. The Severn runs fast and he turned at once towards the Welsh shore and began to swim across the current. In his haste he forgot that he was still wearing a parachute strapped under his buttocks. For twenty minutes he fought the stream in agony, approaching exhaustion. Every movement of his legs brought grinding pain. His arms were soon leaden with weariness, his throat and lungs raw with the rasping of cold air and gritty spray. When, at last, he could touch bottom, he found his legs buckling under him. Three rescuers, wading in to drag him to safety, found him too heavy for them: his parachute, waterlogged, weighed half as much as he did.

When they laid him on dry land he screamed as they tried to lift him. The doctor found that he had broken both legs and seven ribs.

In the Sergeants' Mess, the event was discussed ribaldly; as are all pilot errors. Lacey took a moment off for some sober thought on the fallibility of everyone who handles a fast, lethal machine. If he had to die or be injured in this war it was going to be by enemy action and not his own damned foolishness.

In December, 1939, Fighter Command decided that 501 Squadron was now fully operational and posted it to Tangmere. 601 (County of London) Squadron, AAF, commanded by Loel Guinness and adorned by such other plutocratic names as Whitney Straight and Max Aitken, 'and all the other millionaire boys', was at Tangmere then; along with 92 Squadron; and a mysterious unit which flew Lysanders whose pilots would say nothing about their work. They operated mostly at night, presumably to France, and returned before dawn.

In the third month of war, Tangmere still ran as a well established peacetime station. There was ample provision of servants in both the Officers' and Sergeants' Messes, and Lacey found his uniforms impeccably cleaned and pressed for him. It was the rule that each sergeant had to take it in turn to be mess caterer for a month. Lacey repeats the old Service legend that, 'At the end of the month you were able to buy a car. You more or less had to: there was no other way of getting rid of the money!' With second-hand cars costing from five to twenty pounds, this, even if faintly true, did not represent a vast deal of profiteering.

Christmas at the new, comfortable station brought a welcome break in the boredom of the phoney war. Daily flights over the English Channel, circling convoys monotonously with never a sight of the enemy in the air or on the sea, were discouraging of enterprise.

But Group began to shift the emphasis to night flying: not only was there constant night practice, but a stand-by aircraft was detailed from dusk to dawn.

The Squadron Adjutant's memory was long enough to stretch back three months.

He sent for Lacey.

'Sir?'

'Oh, Sergeant: you have more night flying time in your log-book than anyone else on the squadron, I see.'

'Have I sir?' The authentic look of faintly surprised innocence figured here; rather blighted by the pink veins around the youthful blue pupils, which told of rapid maturity hastened by another late party in the Sergeants' Mess the night before.

'You know damn well you have.'

Silence. *Hell, how the light from that window is hurting my eyes!*

'So,' said the Adjutant, matching the look of frankness with one of his own, 'I'm afraid you're going to find yourself doing duty stand-by pilot most nights.'

This merely entailed sleeping between rather smelly blankets in the hangar, with the aircraft a few yards outside. And every night the Operations Room would telephone a practice scramble. In theory, the duty stand-by pilot then leaped up, buckled on his parachute, sprinted to his cockpit, fastened his straps, put on his helmet and plugged it in to the radio, started the engine and taxied to the end of the runway in use. Meanwhile the Duty Pilot on Flying Control duties, and his crew, were frantically laying a string of flarepath lights. The stand-by pilot then called Ops. on the R/T and was promptly ordered to return to dispersal and switch off. And there ended the practice night scramble.

Familiarity with this frustrating procedure bred a spirit of competition to reduce the time it took to report from the end of the runway. The pilots, when on stand-by at night, left their parachutes and cockpit straps undone and merely plugged their helmets in to the R/T. In consequence, the practice scramble times shrank gratifyingly and became a matter of pride and satisfaction to both Ops. and Group.

One night, when Sergeant Lacey was adorning the role of stand-by pilot and had arrived at the end of the runway in his Hurricane with fantastic smartness, still thinking of the cliff-hanging thriller he had just left and to which he was in a hurry to return, the fruity voice of the Ops. Controller curtly ordered: 'Scramble!'

'Eh?' The exclamation burst from the stand-by pilot before he could restrain himself.

'Scramble!'

'Understand scramble,' acknowledged Sergeant Lacey briskly; and then muttering under his breath he hastily began to repair his omissions in the matter of straps and buckles. He got airborne; eventually.

A big ship, steaming past Beachy Head, was being bombed. By the time Tangmere's stand-by night fighter arrived, the German bomber crews were sitting down to sauerkraut and ersatz coffee, in their own messes in the Vaterland.

Thereafter, night flying stand-by was treated less lightheartedly and scramble times noticeably increased, provoking irascible comment from Group.

Sergeant Lacey withdrew from the conflict temporarily, to have German measles; and to start it on a round of the station. The Station Warrant Officer, who was a notorious xenophobe, cut him for the next month. He might at least have had the decency to contract British measles; especially with a war on.

But spring brought an end to the sceptical mood in which the first six or seven months of the war had passed. During this time the squadron had been settling down together to unfamiliar routine, to the blackout and security-mindedness and all the other phenomena of war. Hitler had left England pretty much unmolested and despite casualties in the air among people whom they knew on bomber squadrons, the home-based fighter squadrons had so far felt rather like privileged participants in a massively organized game. They had the pleasure of greatly augmented flying hours, the sharpened senses that came from knowing that they were technically at war; and no hardship or danger.

In March, the air war for the RAF squadrons in France, which had been quiescent since the previous November, flared up again: fighter to fighter, the RAF fought the Luftwaffe. The German bombers had not yet reappeared in large numbers over France.

News of air battles reaching Tangmere made the pilots impatient to join in.

In April, Blenheims, Wellingtons and Hudsons were in action over north-west Germany and the Heligoland Bight. More news to whet the operational appetites of 501.

At last, in May, the Squadron was warned to prepare to go to France.

Like all momentous events, this one is remembered for its personally significant trivialities. Lacey, reporting to the dentist for examination before going overseas, was told that two teeth needed filling; but there was no time to do this, so they must be extracted. He says that he has missed those two teeth ever since.

Chapter Four

FRANCE

THE RAF squadrons already serving in France were in two formations: the Advanced Air Striking Force, of which the fighter squadrons were Nos. 1 and 73; and the Air Component of the British Expeditionary Force, whose fighter squadrons were Nos. 85, 87, 615 and 607.

On the 10th May 1940, Nos. 3, 79 and 504 Squadrons were sent to reinforce the Air Component, and Nos. 17, 242 and 501 to the Advanced Air Striking Force.

May 10th was a day of crisis: Germany invaded both Holland and Belgium, without formal declaration of war.

The Governments of the Netherlands and Belgium had already received warning of the danger, by means of captured documents and their intelligence services, and had asked Britain for help, particularly in the air, in the event of attack. This had been promised, although it committed the Service which could least be spared.

At dawn, the German Air Force attacked both countries simultaneously with heavy air raids on aerodromes, communications, capital cities and troop concentrations. Within a few hours more than half the aircraft of the Belgian Air Force were destroyed on the ground. At the same time, the German Army advanced strongly on Holland, Belgium and Luxembourg.

At six o'clock in the morning, the Dutch and Belgian Ministers in Paris and London appealed for the promised aid. Within a matter of hours, 501 Squadron was among those ordered to give it.

The reinforcing squadrons sent to France arrived in a setting in which they were at a considerable disadvantage.

German aircraft production had already more than replaced the number of aircraft shot down over Poland, Norway, France and the United Kingdom with its approaches. Thus the Luftwaffe, which was numerically greater at the outbreak of war, was daily growing at a faster rate than British industry could yet attain.

Poland, Denmark and Norway were under enemy occupation, and Russia was bound by a non-aggression pact with Germany. The air forces of Britain's allies were nugatory, by reason of small numbers of inferior aircraft.

The RAF was therefore not only outnumbered but compelled to cover a huge area; and devoid of any prospect that Russia, Italy, America or any other country with a large air force was likely to join the Allies.

At 2.30 PM all sixteen Hurricanes of 501, led by Squadron Leader M. V. M. Clube, took off for Betheniville, near Rheims. The move was completed by 5.15 PM on the next day.

It was hard to believe that they were flying towards places which had, that morning, been the scenes of barbarous holocausts, for there was a certain holiday feeling about the trip. The sparkling sea, the clear sky and the sun warm through their cockpit canopies; the sense of adventure, the feeling of relief that at last they were going to do something more positively concerned with the nation's task of defeating the Germans: all these added up to a heady satisfaction for highly-trained young men. Few of them had been abroad before and the mere anticipation of seeing France, perhaps managing a visit to Paris, was enough to dispel immediate fear and the unavoidable thought that some would almost certainly never see England again.

Sergeant Pilot Lacey, looking down for his first sight of their new base, saw a vast field with a hump in the centre which, he found when they landed, made it impossible to see one side of the aerodrome from the other. Buildings there were none.

With their aircraft parked in a row at one side of the airfield, the pilots stood in a group surveying their new home. 'Not much like Tangmere,' remarked one. Nobody disagreed with him.

'What's the form, sir?' One of the Flight Commanders asked the CO.

The squadron leader pointed towards the edge of the field. 'We'll put up a couple of big tents here as a rest room and

47

an Ops. Room. As soon as the rest of the chaps arrive we'll start pitching tents on the domestic site: that's about a mile from the aerodrome.'

'Call this an aerodrome!' This rueful cry was drowned by the sound of the first of the heavy aircraft that were bringing the squadron's ground crews: two Bristol Bombay troop carriers and an Armstrong Whitworth Ensign airliner.

The first Bombay landed and the Hurricane pilots watched with amusement as it disappeared and then came into sight over the rise in the centre of the field. Then the dignified Ensign, looking markedly outraged by its crudely applied field service camouflage, lumbered in. The other Bombay came over the hedge, and somebody had just said, 'Now they can get cracking with those tents; and a brew up: I could do with some cha,' when silence fell over the watchers.

Mute, holding their breaths, the Hurricane pilots stood with their eyes fixed on the big troop carrier. The ground airmen and officers who had emerged from the first Bombay and the Ensign, and had been calling to one another or chattering loudly with excited comment on their new surroundings, also let their voices drift into silence.

The Bombay which had just flown over the boundary and looked as though it was about to touch down, was climbing again: its nose up at an angle of sixty degrees, it hovered on the edge of a stall. Everybody knew what must happen. Each one of them wanted to shout a fruitless warning to the pilot. Their stomachs taut with the anticipation of what they realized they must witness in the next few seconds, the members of the squadron looked on helplessly.

The Bombay hung, nose-up, for a second or two; then its nose and one wingtip dropped heavily and it spun into the ground with a thud which sent a tremor through the onlookers' feet. The roaring of the engines combined with the thunder of the impact made their hearts leap with shock; then there was silence.

For ten seconds they waited for a tongue of flame; but there was to be no explosion of petrol vapour, no fire. Feet pounded across the turf.

Lacey could see the Adjutant, through a window of the

cabin: although the officer sat motionless, he looked unhurt. When he scrambled into the aircraft, he saw that the Adjutant was indeed unmarked; but had died of a broken neck. Among the nine who were killed in the accident or died in hospital were both ground crew and spare pilots.

It was a hateful, ominous start to the squadron's service in France. In an instant the holiday atmosphere vanished.

Worse was to come. The doleful ceremony of burial next day was not to be the end of this accident. Three nights later there was an air raid: bombs intended for the airfield fell in the nearby cemetery, disinterring the bodies which had so recently been laid there; reburial of the corpses dismembered by bombs was as gory as it was macabre.

This first day had not exhausted its horrors, however. Two hours after landing, while the squadron was busy erecting its tents, a Dornier swept in low and straffed. With machine gun bullets flinging up divots all around them, officers and airmen sprinted away from the line of fire. There was no need for the CO to take any action to enforce his order that slit trenches were to be dug.

But they were here to fly, and singly and in pairs the pilots were sent off on sector reconnaissance and patrols to familiarize themselves with the area as soon as possible that same day.

At once, the squadron was in action.

Flying Officer A. D. Pickup, patrolling 15 miles north-west of Vouziers, intercepted a Do 17 and dived instantly to attack. Two minutes later he saw it hurtling down wreathed in smoke and flames as the pilot jumped clear: he watched the German's parachute open and wondered whether, perhaps, the reception awaiting the latter from the French peasantry might make him wish that he had died with his crew.

The squadron was jubilant. Everyone had a vicarious part in the kill. They all felt that danger and discomfort were amply compensated for. This great event made each man, fitter, rigger or Orderly Room clerk, a fighting member of a fighting unit, added enormously to his morale and seriousness of purpose, and gave a sense of immediacy to the squadron's task.

Every pilot wanted to hear Pickup's story a dozen times

over. Each believed that he could have done as well, given the luck to make the interception. Every one of them burned with impatience for his own chance to come. The day was not long enough and they went to bed longing for the first light that would allow them to fly again and hunt the enemy.

Lacey took off shortly before dusk. He climbed quickly, searching the sky for hostile aircraft and looking down as often as possible to fix landmarks in his mind. When he turned for home, he realized that these big French fields with so few hedges between them were difficult to differentiate between: but he thought that he could identify the aerodrome.

He spiralled down, lowered his undercarriage and landed gently. Then he taxied; and taxied; and taxied. One field gave onto another. And dusk settled. And still there was no sign of the two big tents which would tell him he was back at base.

At last he cut off his engine, got out of his aircraft and began to walk towards the lights which glowed a short distance away.

A voice challenged him from the shadow under a tree. He stopped. He had always wondered whether he would find his school French of any use; now was the time to find out: and quickly, for a steel-helmeted poilu had appeared from the shadow and was pointing a rifle at him. The bayonet looked unpleasantly long and sharp.

'Anglais,' he ventured.

The poilu said something incomprehensible.

'Pilot,' Lacey explained hopefully. 'RAF. Savez-vouse?'

The poilu shouted. Lacey resignedly stood motionless until two more men hurried up. Then, 'Anglais,' he repeated patiently. 'Pilot.'

One of the men, with a corporal's chevrons on his sleeves, approached, stood looking at him like a suspicious pointer and then beckoned. The four of them went to a house on the outskirts of the small village.

When the officer commanding the detachment spoke to him in hesitant but recognizable English, Lacey was so relieved that he would not have seriously resisted an attempt to kiss him on both cheeks.

The French officer put him in touch with his squadron by

telephone; the natives were friendly and their supply of wine and cognac was abundant; with a head throbbing more than a little, Lacey took off at first light and this time he found his way correctly to base.

It had been a late night for Sergeant Pilot Lacey as he contributed his bit to the entente cordiale; he had been celebrating the end of a day that was momentous also for Britain's most distinguished citizen: Mr Winston Churchill had, on the morning of 10th May, been asked by King George VI to form a new Government. The Prime Minister, too, was tardy in going to his bed: at 3 AM, looking forward to the morrow. The squadrons, indeed the whole British force, fighting in France had little time to think about the new premiership; but it was the first step towards victory although the near future held defeat and retreat for them. The news that Churchill was leading the nation was heartening despite the undeniable hopelessness of the immediate situation in Europe.

During the night, the airfield had been the target for an air raid. Lacey landed there to be met by ribald comment on his foreknowledge that had led him to spend the night elsewhere. In fact, the Luftwaffe had missed their objective and it was the village of Betheniville and a few empty meadows which had been hit. The raid had, however, been a salutary encouragement to the more careless airmen to give some thought to their own safety: this, on top of the Dornier's straffing the previous afternoon, had bred a fury of trench digging. Whereas at first the troops had made the excuse, when issued with spades, that they were fully occupied by aircraft maintenance, it was now, for a few hours, impossible to divert them from their excavating long enough to carry out daily inspections on the aircraft.

'It's amazing how bombing changes your outlook,' remarks Lacey.

But he was in no mood to quip during those first three days in France. The other pilots on the squadron were shooting down the enemy, some of them more than one apiece, and he could not even make a start.

On the 11th, he flew twice. At the end of the day, with his score at nil, the squadron had accounted for six hostiles: Pilot

Officer C. L. Hulse and Sergeant P. Morfill a Me 110 each; Flying Officer C. E. Malfroy (the New Zealand Davis Cup player) and Flight Sergeant A. D. Payne each a Heinkel 111; and a Do 17 apiece for Flight Lieutenant E. S. Williams, 'B' Flight Commander, and Sergeant R. C. Dafforn.

On the 12th, Lacey flew three patrols, totalling 3 hours 45 minutes, and still his duck remained unbroken. But his comrades destroyed twelve German aeroplanes. He 111s were brought down by Sergeant P. C. Farnes, Sergeant D. S. Mackay, Sergeant Morfill, Flight Sergeant Payne and Flying Officer P. H. Rayner. Farnes and Pilot Officer E. J. H. Sylvester shared a Do 17 and another was destroyed by Pilot Officer K. N. T. Lee. Flying Officer E. Holden got a Ju 88 and Sergeant J. E. Proctor a Me 110 and a Do 17.

Nobody had yet come up against that formidable enemy fighter, the Me 109.

But it was not entirely a day about which to be glad.

Rayner did not come back from his patrol. Sylvester saw him crash to his death after he had shot down his Heinkel, 30 miles north-east of Betheniville. Flying Officer M. F. C. Smith was killed by a Me 110.

The fat days at Filton and Tangmere, the comfort of permanent billets and the complacent certainty that you and your friends would all be alive tomorrow, seemed a long time ago. You remembered the parties in the mess or in the 'local', and memory flashed a picture before your eyes of a flushed, laughing face and brought back the sound of a voice telling a joke or joining in a song. You felt a tightening of your stomach and you looked quickly around for a drink. Above all, you didn't talk about it.

Then, on the 13th May came the dawn patrol on which Lacey, separated from his companions, shot down a Heinkel 111 and a Messerschmitt 109 within a few minutes of each other; and the second sortie, immediately after he had landed to refuel and rearm, on which he destroyed a Messerschmitt 110 and Griffiths and Lee got two more: and all before breakfast. For this, the French Government bestowed on him a Croix de Guerre.

On the next day he was sent to Mourmelon, a French aerodrome, by road to collect a Hurricane which had been forced landed there by one of the other pilots of 501 and was now fit to be flown.

The transport driver had other duties on his list and Lacey, since he was to fly back to Betheniville straight away, sent the truck on its way. He walked towards the hangar with his parachute slung across his shoulder, looking up at the sky as usual and thinking what a clear day it was. But his Hurricane wasn't in the hangar. He stood outside, searching, and saw it parked on the far side of the airfield among some trees. A French officer gave him permission to walk across the aerodrome; he had hoped for the offer of a lift in a lorry or at least the loan of a bicycle: but he found himself trudging across the grass in his flying boots, lugging the bulky parachute.

He was half-way across, wondering what law of mathematics it is which makes any given distance expand to five times its previously estimated length as one walks it, when he heard a harsh, concerted sound throbbing overhead with ominously increasing volume.

Stopping, he rested the parachute between his feet and stared up, trying to determine the source of the quickly approaching noise; but the roar of engines seemed to fill the air and there was no immediate way of telling whence it came. Until, in a flash, silvery glinting in the sunlight, the aeroplanes swept thunderously into view: twenty Do 17s and twenty Ju 87s.

'I never felt so naked in my life as standing in the middle of that airfield. I didn't mind the hangars and camp which I had just left, being bombed ...' who would, after not having been offered a ride across the big airfield, on a hot day? '... but I did object to the sticks of bombs which were being dropped across the aerodrome, where I was standing. It felt as though every bomb was being aimed individually at me.' He flung himself face down on the warm, friendly-smelling grass, a dandelion tickling his nose until he sneezed; he clasped his arms above his head for some protection and hoped for the best.

A stick of bombs fell only fifty yards away. Each explosion

thudded through his chest and stomach and the two nearest ones lifted him inches from the ground with a sickening sensation. Dust and pebbles and clods of turf spattered around and on him. 'I remember thinking at the time that lightning never strikes the same place twice.' So, as the ground ceased trembling and the shower of earth subsided, he picked himself up with his parachute, sprinted to the edge of the nearest crater and dived into it. Instantly he gave a shout of pain and annoyance as, with a stench of singed serge, he felt himself scorched by a hot shard of bomb casing. For the next three or four minutes, while the Ju 87 dive bombers came screaming down in successive waves, he crawled carefully about the hole in which he was sheltering, trying to find a place where he could lie down without being branded by almost red hot pieces of metal.

But his theory about lightning never striking twice in the same place was vindicated and presently the attacking aircraft were gone and he was still unhurt. Climbing out of his crater, he did not even stop to look at the damage around him; he was conscious of columns of smoke and some haze in the air where dust clouds still hovered over stricken buildings, but there was no time to do a W. H. Davies act: 'What is this life, if full of care, We have no time to stand and stare.' Sergeant Pilot Lacey was, at that moment, very full of care. He took to his heels, more energetically than he had done since his last game of rugger. You never knew when the beggars might be back and he had to get the Hurricane away.

A couple of French mechanics came, grinning, out of hiding among the trees and helped him to start the engine. Then, picking his way among the bomb holes, he took off.

It looked as though he were to be given a special chance to improve his knowledge of French topography, for that evening he was detailed, with four other pilots, to travel by lorry to Villeneuve and collect five new aircraft. His companions were 'Hawkeye' Lee, who had trained with him at Perth, MacKay who had a quick wit, Farnes and someone whose name he cannot remember.

He recalls the journey as the worst he ever made in his life. A three-ton truck does not offer Babylonian luxury, in the first place. Added to this was the fact that their driver was a novice at his job, so the five passengers had to take it in turns to do it for him.

For mile after mile they crawled along in second gear. The road was crowded with refugees. The column of forlorn, suffering men, women and children seemed never-ending as it trudged dumbly on its broken way to God knew where. These people had been moving at their heart-broken, heavy-footed pace for four days. Time and again German aircraft had dived on them to attack with bombs and machine-gun fire. The purpose may have been partly to scare them off the roads and clear the way for the German Army's advance; but nobody had any doubt that the attacks were mainly prompted by deliberate brutality and that perverted German sense of humour that finds amusement in any bullying act.

The five British pilots felt reluctant to sound the horn of their lorry to force a path through this press of miserable humanity. They saw bloody heaps of torn clothes and flesh which were the remains of children slaughtered by the Luftwaffe in unopposed straffing of the road, carried still by their parents on farm-carts laden with old people and a few household goods. Ancient women sat, with their legs dangling over the sides of the carts, keening and praying for safety. Their husbands, shrunken with fear and hunger, muttered dry-throated curses on the enemy who, they knew, would come and come again.

In places the road was jammed across its whole width and the only way to make any progress was gently to nudge the wretched people aside with mudguards and bumpers as the three-tonner crawled ahead in low gear.

Those who were not driving slept in the back of the lorry. Their overpowering tiredness came from their incessant vigilance in the air, the many hours they had to fly each day and the nervous tension which had never left them. Already, after only four days in France, they were having a foretaste of the rigours and weariness of the Battle of Britain.

At last dawn came and Villeneuve was only a few miles distant. The grey light shewed them even more clearly the pathetic picture of suffering and they almost wished that it was dark again. The pinched faces of hungry, terrified children; the sullen resignation of families who stubbornly carted their dead instead of abandoning them in ditches; the hatred in the voices which, when the RAF lorry was recognized, shouted ahead to clear a path and urged the pilots who rode in it to hurry on their way and get on with the work of shooting down *les sales Boches*: these were the pattern of that night and the following dawn, which are printed indelibly on the memory.

Heavy-eyed and stiff, the five of them clambered down from the lorry, found their aircraft, hurriedly checked the harmonization of the guns and the amount of fuel in the tanks, and took off. They had been ordered to carry out a patrol on their way back to base. After what they had seen on the road overnight they were ripe to do some killing. Not fifteen minutes after they were in the air Lacey saw a speck in the sky away to the starboard. He looked at it steadily for a few seconds ... yes ... it was an Me 110.

The five Hurricanes turned towards the solitary enemy aircraft; but its pilot had sharp eyes too. He turned as well, and though they chased him as far as the German frontier, they had to let him go; he was too fast for them. Even so, there was some satisfaction to be had: 'It was nice to be five to one and chasing him.'

It had been an unpleasant night and a disappointing morning. Some food would be welcome. They approached Betheni-ville ...

Lacey flicked on his R/T and called Hawkeye Lee. 'D'you see what I see?'

'I'm afraid I do. Where have the blighters gone?'

For the tented camp had disappeared.

Puzzled and annoyed, they circled the field once, looking for signs of life. They saw someone, shading his eyes, gazing up at them; and as they landed he came running to meet them. Lacey cut his engine and shouted at him from the cockpit.

'What's happened, Corporal?'

'The squadron's gone, Sarge.'

'I can see that. Where to?'

'I don't know. But they went that way.' The corporal pointed southward. 'And they left me here on my own.'

The pilots stood round the corporal, laughing uncertainly and making wry comments. It might take them all day to find the squadron's new base: surely the corporal should have been told where to rejoin them? Anyhow, there was a big dump of petrol in four-gallon cans.

'There's only one thing to do,' said Lacey, 'fill up with petrol and go looking for the squadron.'

But the corporal had other ideas. 'No petrol,' he told them firmly. 'I was given strict orders to burn it all.'

'But you haven't burnt it yet?'

'No. But I was told to burn it *all*. I wasn't told anything about refuelling any aircraft.'

This was commendable conscientiousness and in other circumstances might have been amusing. But after a nightmare journey, a frustrating patrol, and the prospect of a search for the squadron which could have been avoided if someone had used a little common sense, the five tired, hungry pilots gave the corporal short shrift. Euphemistically, Lacey puts it: 'We managed to convince him that he wasn't going to burn any petrol until we had filled our tanks.' This they did, filtering the petrol through a chamois leather. Even so, it was a pity to leave any behind; but they had no way of taking any cans with them. As they climbed away they saw the bright flash and pillar of smoke which told them that the corporal was dutifully obeying orders. What a waste, when tanker crews were being torpedoed and drowned or burned to death almost every day in their efforts to get the precious fuel through.

There were a dozen other airmen who had been left behind to help in packing up the last of the squadron's gear. They, and the few French civilians loitering about the airfield, all claimed that the Germans were 'ten miles down the road'. Before turning south, Lacey and his companions flew back looking for the enemy; not finding him, they set out on their vague search for the rest of 501.

Flying at the most economical cruising speed, they made their fuel last as long as possible; but finally they had to decide on a place where they could land, make inquiries and refuel. The most suitable was Barbery, a military airfield outside Troyes.

Here they were given a cold reception by the Commandant:
'Get your aeroplanes off my airfield as soon as possible.'

'Why?'

'Because if the Germans spot them on the ground they'll
come and bomb us in an attempt to destroy them.'

MacKay looked at Lee, who looked at Lacey. The last, as
spokesman, said: 'That's all very well, but we can't take off
until we have refuelled.'

'You can have some of our petrol. Anything ... only hurry
and go.'

'We can't use your petrol: it's not up to our octane value ...
Sir.'

The Commandant looked as though he wished he had
special powers to send British NCO pilots in front of a firing
squad. Lacey, watching him with his particular brand of
irritating blandness, wondered if the Frenchman would dash
his cap to the ground and jump on it. He didn't do that, but he
did stamp his feet and deliver a tirade of which they did not
understand a single word; although they correctly deduced the
meaning of 'défi' and 'insurbordonné' which recurred frequently. When at last they had convinced the Commandant,
by their silence and the medium of a few commonly understood English phrases, that they were determined not to
pour French petrol into their Hurricanes, he pointed to a
pile of camouflage nets and stalked away talking huffily to
himself.

Doing the decent thing, the sergeants pulled the camouflage netting over their five unwelcome aircraft and left the
camp, to find any sort of British unit.

Two hundred yards from the main gate, they arrived at a
café. Without a word, they crossed the road and seated themselves. They had not eaten since the previous evening.

'We had about a ten-egg omelette each, with asparagus and
rum. And then, when we left, it was such a wonderful day that
we just lay down on the pavement and went to sleep.'

Lacey recalls the meal casually, but the youthfully matter-
of-fact words hide a poignant picture of exhaustion.

When they woke, they spent the rest of the daylight hours
fruitlessly trying to get in touch with some RAF formation.

There was nothing for it, eventually, but to find empty beds in a barrack room on the camp and settle down for the night. It was all very well to expect officers and senior NCOs to use initiative, but this was carrying things a bit too far. Irritants like this were worse for morale than any amount of bombing. They wondered what efforts the squadron was making to find them.

Next morning they learned, with the help of the French Commandant, that 501 was on the small airfield of Allemanche, fifty miles away. They rejoined their unit and flew two patrols that day.

In the meanwhile the other pilots had been increasing their score. On the 14th, Flying Officer J. D. Cridland shot down a Do 17, Flight Sergeant Payne and Sergeant Dafforn each a He 111, and Sergeant Proctor two of the latter. On the 15th, Do 17s were destroyed by Flight Lieutenant Griffiths and Flight Sergeant Payne, and a Me 110 by Sergeant Proctor. Pilot Officer Lindsell and Pilot Officer C. Hancock, who were on their way between Rheims and Betheniville by car, picked up the pilot of Griffiths's victim after he had baled out. Cridland and Pilot Officer Hairs together engaged another Do 17 at 10,000 feet, and after the former had silenced its rear gunner, they saw the bomber spinning down with its fuselage in flames and smoke pouring from both engines; but as they did not see it hit the ground and no report of this was received, they were denied a confirmed victory.

The Do 17 pilot whom Lindsell and Hancock brought back to camp did the squadron a lot of good. Sitting in surly silence as they drove up to the dispersal point, the German refused any overtures of kindness. When offered a cigarette he refused it with a curt remark of which they guessed the gist by its contemptuous tone and the twist of his mouth. When he saw the hard-working, but unmilitarily untidy fitters and riggers around the Hurricanes, he laughed openly and commented again. By the time he had been taken into the Operations tent, all the pilots and most of the ground crews had seen him: nothing could have been better calculated than his arrogance, to bring home to them the misery that awaited Britain if the Nazis won the war.

That German prisoner was paradoxically the best public relations man the unit could have encountered.

On the 17th May, by which time Lacey felt as though he had been in France for a year instead of a week, he attacked German armour for the first time. On the second patrol of the day his section saw a long line of Panzer Mk III tanks streaming along the road. Going down steeply, they opened fire with their .303 machine-guns. 'It was like shooting at elephants with a pea-shooter. The tank commanders didn't even pay us the compliment of closing their turrets: they just ducked their heads as we came over and stuck them out again as soon as we'd gone past. The tanks rolled on completely undamaged.'

Such was the war for 501 Squadron during the next ten days. They were under canvas again and in some respects their life on campaign was much the same as it had been for their grandfathers in the Boer War forty years earlier. But, though their living conditions were crude, their morale was good; and they had with them still some reminders of the good life on permanent home stations: someone still had to be Mess Caterer and do the Sergeants' Mess marketing between operational flights, for instance.

Weariness was ever-present. Pilots and mechanics both took advantage of every opportunity to stretch out on the grass or in a battered deck-chair and snatch a few minutes' sleep between intervals of work. Whoever had to go into Sezanne or the neighbouring villages to buy food with which to supplement issue rations, welcomed the break from the always imminent call to scramble or to lend an extra pair of hands to repair a Hurricane damaged by flak or the bullets of an enemy aircraft's machine-guns.

Anti-aircraft fire was a daily increasing menace. As the Germans swept across France and the British bombers and fighters operated more over enemy-held territory, the flak sites seemed to multiply with the indestructible fertility of cancer cells. Every time the squadron flew, now, they had to dodge the flak bursting around them with unnerving accuracy. First there would be the grey puffs of smoke opening out like dandelion seed; then they would look down and see the wicked red and yellow flashes from the heart of a coppice or the shelter of a farmyard wall, where the gun sites were. A few seconds later the billows of smoke from the bursting shells would be closer, there would be a thud as a sliver of metal struck a wing or fuselage; the air would be made turbulent as salvos burst in quick succession. For a few seconds the effect was mesmerizing: the apparently lazy approach of the flickering trail of tracer; then the dreadful moment when it flashed past with astonishing speed and you knew that it had been aimed at you and barely missed.

One morning, when the squadron was operating in full strength, the twelve Hurricanes flew into a barrage of anti-aircraft fire so intense that the air around them boiled with the viciousness of a storm cloud. The pilots felt violent gusts of air snatch and drag at the control surfaces. Lacey, flying as Yellow Leader, saw Flight Sergeant Payne's aircraft, ahead of him in the Red Three position, flung into an involuntary half roll. It dropped like a stone for a couple of hundred feet and as Lacey struggled to hold his own machine level he saw the other slowly roll out to level flight and clamber up to position again. The turbulence created by the flak had been enough to toss the fighter completely upside down despite its pilot's effort to hold it steady.

Pilot Officer Sylvester did not return from this patrol, after having been last seen diving on a gun site. He turned up the next day, and reported having forced landed: badly shot up by a Do 17 he was attacking and by heavy AA guns, he had lost his bearings.

Even among operational fighter pilots there are some who are not cast in a heroic mould. Lacey recalls one of the squadron who, from the first, betrayed a marked reluctance to fly when there was danger of being shot at, either by flak or enemy aircraft. During one of the air raids on one of the fields from which 501 operated in France, Lacey, caught as usual with his pants figuratively down, took to his heels in what he claims was better than Olympic 100 metres time. There was no one else in sight at the moment that he began to run for shelter, and as he hurled himself into a slit trench he supposed it could have no other occupant. He was immediately disillusioned by a grunt and the smell of tobacco. Having landed face-down, in a sprawl, it took him a moment or two to ease into a more collected position; then, looking round, he saw that he had a companion: steel-helmeted, leaning comfortably against the end wall of the trench as he sat on a cushion, smoking a pipe, was the reluctant pilot – reading a newspaper! Lacey thinks he must have gone there directly after breakfast. It was then about lunch time . . .

On the 19th, Lacey led a section ordered to patrol for enemy fighters. The flak was heavy and accurate and the language on the R/T reflected the section's feelings as the leader twisted and shifted altitude. His sharp eyes spotted three He 111s just south of Rheims and for a moment, as his Number Two drew his attention to what he had already seen, Lacey was tempted to tear into them. But he reluctantly reminded himself that they were looking for fighters, and left the bombers alone in the hope that someone else would deal with them. It was a great temptation to forsake the patrol temporarily and tackle the target of opportunity: but with only fifteen seconds' worth of ammunition in a Hurricane's guns, it might have meant sacrificing the chance of attacking enemy fighters later.

On 27th May the squadron was ordered to operate for the day from a forward airfield, near Rouen, quaintly named Boos.

The situation by then was grim. Boulogne had fallen four days earlier and, only the day before, Calais had been taken after a desperate defence. The Belgian Army, on a front eight miles west of Ghent, was fighting with doomed gallantry on the point of capitulation. Dunkirk had been subjected to massive air raids. The British Expeditionary Force was being squeezed out of France, threatened by annihilation.

Scarcely had 501 landed at Boos than 'the sky was black with He 111s, about fifty of them; and once again we got exactly the same treatment as I'd had at Mourmelon.'

There was no petrol in the aircraft for there had not been time to begin refuelling. Unable to taxi or take off, the pilots ran for whatever cover was available. Lacey was a few yards from a big hole in the ground and he jumped into it, to be joined a few seconds later by a tall, hefty, shock-haired flying officer from 73 Squadron which was also on this advanced aerodrome. He recognized his companion: 'Cobber' Kain, one of the earliest fighter DFCs of the war and, at that time, a household name as one of the top-scoring fighter pilots of the day.

Kain won the first DFC of the war to be awarded to a pilot serving in France and had set up a new altitude record for air fighting, by shooting down a Do 17 at 27,000 ft, on the 2nd November 1939. He always wore a Maori good-luck charm pinned to the chest of his white flying sweater and was the most typical of pre-war fighter boys: full of inimitable panache and good humour, with genuine modesty about his exploits. He always maintained that the publicity given to him was on account of his New Zealand nationality and aimed at maintaining Commonwealth morale and stimulating recruiting in the Dominions. He said that 'Fanny' Orton, who was shooting down even more of the enemy than he, should have been the victim of all the fuss and Press adulation. Had he lived, he would surely have been the greatest name in the annals of Fighter Command, surpassing even the many who fought so brilliantly then and later and lived to enjoy the victory won by their bravery and determination.

He was killed soon after, with seventeen successes to his credit, when attempting a roll too near to the ground as he came in to land after shooting down his last German aircraft. He and Lacey sat on oil drums, feverishly chain-smoking, while the ground trembled and pieces of earth tumbled from the sides of the pit. The raid seemed to go on for an inordinately long time but no bombs fell near them as the attack was directed at the hangars on the far side.

Presently the din of bomb bursts subsided, the growl of aero engines faded and silence fell. Kain got up and tossed his cigarette stub aside. 'The party's over.'

Lacey stood up slowly, looking around. 'Seems like it. I wonder what this place is, we've been sitting in?'

Kain glanced about, then, looking at a crudely painted sign-board, did a double take, and with a sudden laugh pointed at it. 'Look at that.'

Lacey looked and felt his knees turn to jelly.

Throughout the heavy raid they had been sitting with some complacence in the main petrol dump.

None of the Hurricanes had been damaged and as soon as they were refuelled the squadron took off.

Within ten minutes they saw a cluster of small crosses approaching, which, when they had covered another few miles, became thirty He 111s, escorted by twenty Me 110s. Whether the latter saw the Hurricanes and decided not to join battle with them, or whether they were only briefed to escort the bombers so far, they executed a lazy 180-degree turn and headed back towards Germany.

'After that it was just a copybook exercise.' 'A' Flight went in first, in two sections of three of which Hawkeye Lee led the first (Red), and Lacey the second (Yellow).

Yellow Section watched, incredulously, as the Heinkels flew straight and level while Red Section opened out and selected the last three bombers in the big formation. There was plenty of time to take in the details. The He 111s were painted very dark green with a white letter on top of the starboard wing. The Germans were taking no evasive or defensive action. The whole scene was being carried out with the unhurried dignity of a practice.

Lacey saw smoke drift back from Lee's guns. A few seconds later there was a loud thudding on his own aircraft and he jerked upright in his straps. He was being shot at! But from where? By whom? A glance over his shoulder only heightened the mystery: despite the sound and feel of strikes on his wing, no holes were appearing; but the wings were being dented. Looking forward again, striving to locate the source of the fire which was evidently aimed at him, he involuntarily pulled his head back and blinked as something hurtled into his windscreen and struck it with noisy force.

Then he recognized what was happening. He was flying through the empty cartridge cases and belt links which were being thrown out of Hawkeye Lee's guns. He climbed quickly so as to avoid this hail of spent ammunition.

By now the He 111s were breaking but offering no return fire. Throughout the engagement Lacey saw no fire from their rear guns. He closed with one which was breaking to the right and braced himself for the expected tracer from the rear turret, his right foot in the strap of the rudder bar, his left tapping the floor. The Heinkel momentarily pulled up and then put its nose down in a diving turn to starboard. He followed it, waiting for the instant when he could get a good shot. The German jinked hard to port and as he crossed the Hurricane's nose Lacey gave him a two-second burst, turning with him. He felt a shock wave of air buffet him as another Hurricane rushed past, putting him off aim. Holding his fire, he saw a flame creep out of the He 111's port engine. Smoke seeped after it. He opened his throttle and closed to fifty yards. The bomber was flying with its port wing tip low. He could see right into the enemy's cockpit through the perspex. The pilot turned to look at him and the last thing the German must have seen was eight blue and orange flashes at the Hurricane's gunports. As Lacey pulled up to avoid colliding with his victim, he saw that the whole of the front part of the aircraft was on fire and, with both engines stopped, it was dropping vertically.

But there was still a lot more trade around and he whipped into a steep climbing turn. There, five hundred feet above him, was a Heinkel sneaking off on its own. He could see the white-edged black crosses on its wings and fuselage and he kept his eyes fixed on them as they grew bigger and nearer. With a few precautionary glances in his mirror and out through his perspex canopy, just in case the fighters had returned, he short-ened the range. And still there was no fire from the rear guns.

He fired with careful deliberation into the starboard engine until the propeller flew off in a myraid shards of metal. The nacelle, wrenched half out of the wing, was smothered in flame. He fired again, shifting his aim to the fuselage, and the bomber staggered into a deep sideslip; a few seconds later two figures scrambled out and parachutes opened while the He 111 fell, inverted, into a small bank of cloud.

Landing back at base, the squadron found that, without any losses, it had shot down fourteen He 111s. 'We'd have des-troyed the lot if our ammunition had lasted out.'

The excursion to Boos had an amusing sequel. Soon after returning to Mourmelon, Sergeant MacKay spotted three approaching specks in the sky. Not intending to be caught on the ground again during an air raid, he dashed to his Hurricane and took off. The specks, when overhead, were identified as French Potez fighters. Sergeant MacKay landed.

The CO, who had been talking to MacKay and some others, asking them about the day's operations, in which he had not taken part, was not pleased by the sergeant's swift reaction to alarm; it was, to say the least, impolite to break off a conversation.

'What the hell d'you mean by taking off without permission, Sergeant MacKay?'

Mac's quick wit was almost his undoing. 'I'm afraid, sir, it was the after effects of . . . of Boos!'

After which retort the CO was even less pleased.

Chapter Five

THE FALL OF FRANCE

LACEY says 'We had a wonderful time in France.' This is not because, looking back after twenty-two years, the small pleasures and the compensations for discomfort appear magnified. Moving from one airfield to another, sleeping and eating always in tents or barns, washing and shaving in cold streams, none of this was a severe hardship in fine weather. There was also the interest, when it was his turn to be Mess Caterer, of finding his schoolboy French improve as he haggled at some market stall or farmer's door, for vegetables, eggs and chickens.

There was the fun of going into a strange town or village to find an estaminet where the wine and the company were good; the satisfactory feeling that, at the end of the day, one had achieved something useful by patrols and combats, after the stultifying winter months in England. The larger picture of the war was gloomy, with Dunkirk under siege and the bulk of the BEF withdrawing within its perimeter to quit France altogether. But the life and work of the squadron went on rather apart from the great tragedy, and fighter pilots are not by temperament given to introspection or a serious consideration of General Staff tactics.

501 Squadron moved to Le Mans. The first night, they slept in the pits on the Grand Prix course; but the CO decided that these were too close to the airfield and too much in the open, so the next day they set up their tents further up the course, in the woods.

Le Mans was a lively town, full of good bars and restaurants, dance halls, cinemas and music halls. The squadron made generous use of it at the end of each day when their patrols were over.

Lacey and Sergeant MacKay, who was a particularly good companion because he had worked in a French bank and spoke the language well, decided one night that it was too late to return to camp. They were not on the roster for an early patrol the next morning, and having dined and wined exceptionally well they felt that it would be fitting to end their evening's enjoyment with a comfortable night's sleep in a hotel bed.

Le Mans was crowded with monied folk who had fled from the path of the German advance, and the hotels were full. After having tried at three or four, the two sergeants decided to walk the town for a while and try to find any humble pension or lodging house that would take them in.

At length, trudging a side street, they saw lights gleaming through a homely, cheerful, brightly patterned chintz curtain.

'This is it,' said MacKay.

'I think we're in luck at last,' agreed Lacey.

They rang the bell. Almost at once the door opened and a severely dressed but smiling woman of about fifty welcomed them in.

'We want two beds for the night,' MacKay explained.

'Mais bien sûr, mon Sergeant. And do you prefer blondes or brunettes? Tall or short? Plump or slim?'

MacKay looked sideways at Lacey, who was grinning broadly, and hesitated. 'Well ... Madame ... my friend and I ...'

'I understand: you would like to see for yourselves ...'

'No, no. Please ... don't inconvenience yourself, Madame ...'

'Ah, les braves Anglais. Toujours la politesse, eh? Come, mes amis ... don't be shy ... I will shew you the young ladies. ...'

She turned away, took a few paces and saw that the two pilots were standing resolutely by the door.

'No need to be shy, boys ...'

'It's not that, Madame. You see ... we have had a late evening ... several bottles of wine ... you know how it is ... we are very tired and we just want a good night's sleep.'

'You can certainly be sure of that!'

'You don't understand, Madame: we simply want beds for the night. Nothing more.'

'But all my beds are already occupied by my young ladies, Sergeant.' She gave them a winning smile of encouragement.

'Then, Madame, perhaps you would be so good as to ask one of the young ladies to give up her bed and sleep with one of the other young ladies: then my friend and I can share her bed. . .'

Lacey and MacKay recoiled before the outraged advance of their would-be landlady. Her face angrily flushed, her inviting tones replaced by a harsh voice of markedly indelicate reproof, she thrust them aside and flung the door open, pointing dramatically into the night-dark street. 'I never heard such a thing. The very idea! I'll have you know I'm running a respectable house . . .'

So the two sergeant pilots had a long walk home.

In this vein of alternating drama and comedy, the last days of the battle for France dragged on. Another 501 pilot, Pilot Officer A. J. Claydon, was killed in action. The squadron patrolled as usual, from dawn to dusk, and sometimes gave escort to bombers sent to attack roads and bridges, railway lines and troop concentrations.

The Fairey Battles operating from French bases had suffered badly from the earliest days of the war. Single-engined aircraft with a top speed of only 250 mph, they carried little defensive armament and made most of their attacks at a dangerously low level.

Lacey, attending a briefing with some of the Battle crews one day when he was leading two sections which were to escort them, gave vein to his macabre sense of humour in a way which brought the most twisted of smiles to the bomber boys' faces. Everybody was ready to leave the briefing tent, except the Battle navigators, who were busy over their charts.

'Hurry up chaps,' Lacey urged them, 'it's time we were going. What are you doing, anyway?'

'Shan't be a minute. We're just working out our courses home.'

'What for? You don't think you're coming back, do you?'

Unfortunately, only about half of them ever did from any raid.

Although this is essentially a story of fighter operations, and particularly the story of one man's war, the achievements of the Fairey Battle squadrons deserve mention in any book that treats of the 1939–40 war in France. It is perhaps enough to say that the first two Victoria Crosses awarded to the RAF in the Second World War, went to Flying Officer D. E. Garland (pilot) and Sergeant Gray (navigator) of No. 12 Squadron, flying Battles. And these were posthumous awards.

There was, indeed, good reason for the scrupulous working out of navigational details before a raid, which always provoked such ribald, macabre comment from the fighter pilots: the Battles had no time to lose in finding their targets. This was demonstrated in the famous attack on the Vroenhoven and Veldwezelt bridges across the Albert Canal, in which these two Victoria Crosses were won, on 12th May 1940.

Blenheims attacked the bridges first, early in the morning, and were fought off by appallingly heavy anti-aircraft fire; but they bombed; and then enemy fighters attacked them. Four Blenheims were shot down and every one of the eight which survived was damaged. The bridges still stood.

No. 12 Squadron, stationed at Amifontaine, was only a hundred miles away and the closest squadron in the Advanced Air Striking Force to the target. Six crews were wanted, everybody on the squadron volunteered and the choice was made by lot. Garland (nicknamed 'Judy' in the Service, after the young film star), who was twenty-one years old, led the raid.

Soon after taking off, one of the Battles had to turn back with a fault in its engine. The remainder, escorted by six Hurricanes, formed two sections.

Eight Hurricanes of No. 1 Squadron flew into the target area first, to try to clear it of enemy fighters. They met a hundred of them, Me 109s, Arados and He 112s, shot down ten, and lost two of their own aircraft although the pilots survived.

The first three Battles, led by Garland, managed to drop their bombs and hit one bridge; but were caught by German fighters as they turned for home, and shot down. The second section of two was intercepted, twenty-five miles from the target, by thirty Me 109s which their three escorting Hurricanes immediately attacked. They bombed the second bridge, hit it and were fired on by a flak barrage of terrible intensity which riddled both bombers.

Of the five Battle Crews on this mission, only one (pilot, navigator and bomb aimer) lived; and even so, Pilot Officer Davy, the captain, had to land at Brussels in an aircraft that burst into flames on touching down.

Good reason, this sort of work, for careful preparation by the navigators; but the escorting fighter pilots, who were themselves taking formidable chances every day, showed no reverence for it; nor were they expected to.

On 9th June, Lacey was in a section flying over Le Havre when they encountered five Me 109s. Instantly, the two formations broke up in a dogfight that scattered them all over the sky. He fired four or five times at two different aircraft, but saw only a few strikes on the tail of one and on the wingtip of the other. It was an inconclusive, desultory affair, with the Germans showing a reluctance to stay. Within three minutes Lacey found himself alone. As he had not been leading the formation, he had no maps with him and when he turned in the direction of Le Mans he had no exact idea of what his course should be.

Some five minutes later he noticed that the temperature of his engine was rising and the oil pressure dropping; there was also an unpleasant clatter from under the cowling, at irregular intervals. While he flew along, searching for a landmark, the engine surged and the whole aircraft shook. A moment later it faltered and he felt the aircraft's nose drop disconcertingly. He knew then that he must have been hit in the engine and that he would have to look for a suitable place on which to make a forced landing.

He soon saw one. A huge, flat plain 'big enough to land the *Queen Mary* on, if you could have got her airborne'. He came down thankfully and lowered his undercarriage.

Congratulating himself on his good luck, judging nicely the moment when he would set the wheels down, he let the aircraft sink gracefully to the ground.

A giant hand grabbed the landing wheels, sucked them into the mushy surface of the marsh on which he had come down, and wrenched the shuddering aircraft to a violent halt that dragged it on to its nose and somersaulting on to its back.

Flung forward into his traps so that his head hit the instrument panel, then thrust against the back rest of his seat so that all the air was driven from his lungs, and finally left suspended upside down with his head in a whirl and his stomach churning, Lacey cursed the treachery of the smooth, boggy field that had beckoned him so alluringly. His ears smarted in the heavy silence after the loud throb of his engine.

For several seconds he hung motionless, gathering his senses. First of all he became aware that water was seeping through the cockpit canopy as the aircraft sank slowly into the soggy earth. He had a vision of drowning, trapped in the inverted cockpit. Next, a loud hissing came to his ears; he recognized that: petrol dripping from his carburettors, over the hot engine. This galvanized him. Struggling furiously with his harness straps, he struggled around so that he was no longer upside down although he now had his feet on the roof of his cockpit hood and his head a few inches from the floor, near the rudder bar. Easing his way forward he found that he was in about eighteen inches of water and cold panic gripped him with the certainty that he was trapped here to drown.

A nauseating wave of claustrophobia washed through him and he flung himself against the side of the perspex, trying to batter a way out with his fists and feet. His head throbbing

71

from the crisp blow it had received as his Hurricane tumbled on to its back, his mind confused with anger and fear of a vile death, he flung himself again and again at the perspex through which he could tantalizingly see the bright sunlight shining on the world outside. He kicked at the transparent panes, but his soft flying boots were of no avail; and he could never have made a hole big enough to crawl through.

And all the while the water was rising. And as it rose, reducing the air space, more petrol fumes were swirling into the cockpit.

With his mind a confusion of thoughts about drowning, being burned to death when the petrol vapour exploded, or dying of asphyxiation, he lost consciousness.

'The next thing I knew was that I was lying flat on my back, in water, looking up into the face of a delightful French girl. The only thing that crossed my mind was, "where on earth did I find her?" I struggled up into a sitting position, but she hurled herself at me and pushed me flat again.'

Lacey ventured a few slow words of French, trying to convince her that he was unhurt; but she kept telling him to lie still. He passed his hands over his body, moved his legs cautiously, and could find no sign of damage. His head ached a bit, but that was all. Yet the pretty French girl would not allow him to sit up.

Over her shoulder appeared the head and shoulders of a British Army corporal. Relieved at the arrival of a fellow countryman, Lacey began to push himself upright once more. To his annoyed astonishment, the corporal pounced and shoved him flat again.

'I'm all right, Corporal . . .'

'Of course you'll be all right, Sarge. You just lie there a minute and we'll fix you up.' The chiding tone reserved for children and imbeciles was meant as solicitude for a sick man, but it did nothing for Sergeant Lacey's good temper.

Still, he had been in worse situations than being so carefully looked after by an attractive French girl.

Presently more helpers arrived, he heard English voices and saw RAF uniforms. Many hands lifted him gently on to a gate and bore him a good half mile to the road, where he was put in an ambulance belonging to No. 12 Squadron, whose Fairey Battles he had escorted on various occasions.

Before they moved off, he had caught a glimpse of his aircraft. The enthusiastic French farm workers who had released him had cut it almost in half with hacksaws and wire cutters in order to do so. 'They did far more damage to that aeroplane than ever the Germans had done!'

Half an hour later he was at 12 Squadron's aerodrome, complaining to the Medical Officer. 'What's all this nonsense about? I'm perfectly all right.'

The MO had an effective, if brutal way of dealing with recalcitrant patients. 'Do you think so?' he asked mildly, reaching for a mirror which he held in front of Lacey's eyes.

Lacey was transfixed by the hideous mask of congealed blood confronting him, through which he barely recognized his own features. 'After that, I didn't feel quite so all right.'

He lay, in a state of shock, while his helmet was soaked off. He had been trapped in the crashed aircraft for an hour and a half and the blood had hardened, fixing the helmet firmly to his head. All the time that the doctor was easing it away from his hair and scalp, Lacey was wondering what appalling injury would be revealed.

He heard the MO grunt as the helmet came away; he felt light fingers swabbing his head and parting his hair, feeling his scalp.

'Well,' said the doctor after a minute, 'all you've got is a gash about half an inch long. It's been bleeding all this time, and the blood has been trickling all over your face. Nothing worse than that.'

Nonetheless Lacey was kept in No. 1 Medical Receiving Station for four days while the doctors watched him for signs of concussion. He was discharged only when the German advance forced the evacuation of the medical receiving station and he was put in charge of an ambulance.

Three hours along the road towards the hospital to which the unit was moving, he saw 501 Squadron's Hurricanes parked on the airfield and knew that he was at Le Mans. Stopping the ambulance, he told the driver to report that he had returned to his squadron and said good-bye.

He was just in time to fly with the squadron to Caen, from which base they carried out a day's patrols. Then back to Le Mans to pack up and move, on 15th June, to Dinard.

The evacuation of Dunkirk had been completed eleven days earlier and the curtain was coming down on operations in France.

For three days they flew their patrols from Dinard, tired and dispirited; depressed by the news of the French defeat and worried about what the future held for Britain.

On the fourth day Lacey was given a day off and went into Dinard to try to get himself a good lunch. When he returned, he found that the squadron had been ordered to Jersey and had gone without him. Hastily packing what he could of his belongings, he found an abandoned car and drove to St Malo. Here he found a potato boat about to sail for the Channel Islands. It was named the *Fairfield*, which was appropriate because that was the name of the house in which he had been born.

After two days in Jersey, doing little and soured by the shattering success of the German blitzkrieg, 501 Squadron returned to England.

There was one compensation. The NAAFI was evacuated just before the squadron took off, and had to abandon much of its stock. The Hurricanes returned to England carrying as many bottles of brandy and cartons of cigarettes as could be stuffed into every odd corner.

'It provided some of the cheapest drinking and smoking I have ever enjoyed.'

They landed at Tangmere to refuel. It was strange to think that only five weeks before they had set out from here, untried; and now they had returned with enough memories and experiences to last a lifetime: hardened campaigners who would look henceforth with a sense of exclusiveness on other men who had not shared the rigours of those famous days; seasoned warriors who had destroyed forty-five enemy aircraft. Of these, Sergeant Pilot Lacey had accounted for five confirmed; and he had been mentioned in dispatches.

'On top of our scooping the abandoned NAAFI stocks, without benefit of payment or Customs Duty, the authorities were very kind to us: they gave us three days' leave to make up for the time we had spent in France. They were very generous in those days!'

Chapter Six

THE BATTLE OF BRITAIN

CROYDON had a special appeal to someone who had been an aviation enthusiast for almost as long as he could remember. It was from here that most of the great British aerial journeys had begun and this was the airport best known to the famous pilots of the world. The centre of British civil flying, Croydon had a permanent place in the history of Imperial Airways and the opening up of Empire and world routes, as well as a constant hold on the affections of aviators like Sir Alan Cobham, Jimmy Mollison, Amy Johnson, Charles Scott and Campbell Black. It was a nostalgic privilege to be guarding Britain from such a base.

Squadron Leader Clube had been posted, as a wing commander, and Flight Lieutenant Griffiths, Flight Lieutenant Williams and Flying Officers Malfroy and Cridland were posted from the squadron too. The new CO was Squadron Leader H. A. V. Hogan, and Flight Lieutenants G. E. B. Stoney and 'Pan' Cox were Flight Commanders.

The sergeant pilots of No. 501 Squadron were housed in the control tower. What they lacked in domestic comfort they made up for during frequent and extended visits to the 'Greyhound' hard by. The kindness of the manager took a practical form: most of them had bank accounts, but after so many months away from home, in the Service, and having lost much of their kit in France, few of them could find cheque books. The landlord accepted cheques made out on the backs of menus or beer mats, as long as they bore a twopenny stamp.

Not one of these was returned to him marked 'Refer to Drawer'.

On the 4th July, after barely a fortnight at Croydon during which they flew uneventful patrols and, in the intervals, put in long hours of sleep and unhurried conviviality, the squadron moved to Middle Wallop, in Hampshire, six miles outside Andover on the Salisbury road; the assault on Britain would come from every direction, and fighter airfields everywhere could expect to be fully committed. Immediately on arrival they were put on Night Readiness.

The pace of the aerial war was quickening. Having begun in May with a few light air raids, by both night and day, the Germans were already sending over as many as a hundred bombers at a time. Enemy aircraft appeared over Britain almost every day and on most nights. So far they had done little damage, but few had been shot down.

The first requirement of an adequate fighter defence was sufficiently early warning of the raiders' approach. Radar stations had been built around our coasts some three years before the outbreak of war, but their coverage was as yet limited and in order to make effective use of the system standing fighter patrols were maintained. In consequence of radiolocation (the contemporary name for radar), the comparatively small British fighter force was able to puzzle the Germans by appearing in whatever area the latter approached.

Night fighting was still in its infancy. It was long before the days of two-man Beaufighters and Mosquitoes with airborne radar operated by the navigator. It was not yet the era of experiment with 'Turbinlight' Havocs: a variant of the fast Boston light bombers, which carried a blindingly powerful searchlight in the nose with which to illuminate enemy bombers; they operated in company with a Hurricane, which flew two hundred yards astern and to starboard, ready to dart ahead and shoot down the target held in the Turbinlight's glare. The Control and Reporting System still operated without the refinement of close control from a radar screen, and fighter controllers were able only to place their fighters in a position of advantage from which they could see the enemy before being seen themselves. At night, all a controller could hope to do was to guide the night fighter towards a searchlight cone which held a hostile aircraft, or close enough to see exhaust flames or a silhouette against cloud.

Hurricanes operating at night were crude instruments in a method of night operating which was perforce unsophisticated.

Middle Wallop had just been built, the living quarters were comfortable, the countryside was beautiful and there were many good pubs within easy reach. All the squadron needed to fill its cup was lots of action: and this it did not get. On most days, the pilots flew down to Warmwell, on the south coast, carried out a couple of patrols from there and returned to their home base in the evening. Even so, the squadron lost a pilot, during one of these routine, uneventful patrols: Sergeant Dixon, covering a convoy off Portland Bill, had to bale out with engine trouble and was drowned. In those days, British fighter pilots did not carry dinghies, and had to rely on their inflatable 'Mae West' life jackets to keep them alive and afloat when they came down in the sea. It was not until a German one-man dinghy was captured, that Britain was able to design one – and better – for the RAF.

This monotony continued until 20th July.

On that afternoon, while the pilots were sunning themselves outside their dispersal hut, a panic call came from the Ops. Room.

When they were airborne the controller told them that a convoy was being attacked near Jersey. In fact, they came upon it only half-way between Portland Bill and the Channel Islands.

First they saw the swarm of steeply diving Ju 87s; and then the escorting Me 109s were upon them.

The leader's R/T crackled 'Tallyho!' and as Lacey broke he quickly sought his first target. Two hundred yards dead ahead, a Messerschmitt was turning towards him. The Hurricane could easily turn inside a Me 109 and Lacey banked hard over, watching the German pilot try to bring his guns to bear. As the 109 flashed by, fifty yards ahead, the Hurricane opened fire. The German twisted down and away; then Lacey followed, waiting for the next chance. Again the Me 109 tried to turn inward and once more Lacey turned with him, holding

77

the inside position. Sharply, the German pulled up and stall turned in the opposite direction. Lacey put a long burst into his fuselage, just astern of the cockpit. The 109 dived sharply, attempting to get away by sheer speed. Lacey opened the taps and held him in his sights at a hundred and fifty yards, pouring another four-second burst into him; this time it was the engine that he hit.

'I can clearly remember watching him slanting down the sky at a hell of a steep angle. A beautiful little blue and grey mottled aircraft with white and black crosses standing out startlingly clear, getting smaller and smaller; and thinking what a terribly small splash he made when he went straight into the Channel.'

Neither on this occasion nor on any other did he feel any compassion for the pilot. It did not occur to him as a fight between himself and another man, but as a totally impersonal combat between two aircraft. Moreover, in his philosophy then, as now, human life was only a speck of dust in the universe and not worth worrying about greatly.

Now he saw another Me 109 about three-quarters of a mile away, flying due north. 'I thought, "Well, he's making a fool of himself. He's going due north. He'll have to turn any moment now and then I've got him." He pulled up in a climbing turn to starboard and I remember thinking he looked exactly like the other one: a beautiful blue and grey mottled effect with the sun shining on him from the south. As he pulled up in a climbing turn I pulled up inside him and as he came into my sights I was giving him an enormous amount of deflection because it was almost a ninety-degree crossing. Then as his turn continued, and I was reducing the deflection, I could see him coming back towards me; I thought for one awful moment that he was going to attempt to crash into me. Then I suddenly saw the aeroplane almost stagger as my bullets were hitting it. It didn't catch fire or break up or anything like that. Its propeller just started to slow down until I could almost see it turning over. Probably the engine had stopped and it was just windmilling. We flashed past each other, a few feet apart, going in opposite directions; and by the time I had whipped round, my new flight commander, "Pan" Cox, latched on to this 109: he didn't fire until he was in to about twenty yards: and once again the dive of that 109 got steeper and steeper and it went in almost right beside the oily patch marking the place where my first one had gone in. I put no claim in for the half-share in that because it was "Pan" Cox's first success. I was getting a bit blasé by that time,' Lacey adds deprecatingly. But, although this statement would qualify for entry in any squadron's 'Line Book', it reflects a genuine lack of egocentricity. There is, too, an unexpected touch of aestheticism in his appreciation of the form and colour values of his two victims on the bright summer's day.

Pilot Officer Sylvester was missing after this action; and this time, he did not turn up again.

Three days later 'a rather amusing incident occurred'. Lacey took off from Middle Wallop on a night patrol. After being vectored all over the sky by the controller, he unexpectedly saw a Heinkel 111 caught in the searchlights some two miles ahead and slightly above; so he started to climb after it. Immediately, some of the searchlights switched to the Hurricane.

Pilots identified themselves by flashing the Letters of the Day on their downward identification lights, if they were fighters, or firing Very light Colours of the Day if they were bombers.

Lacey strained his memory a little, recollected the correct letters and dutifully flashed them on his downwards light. Watching the Heinkel, he saw a red and then a green Very light burst just above it. Much to his surprise the searchlights holding the hostile aircraft at once switched over to his Hurricane. Ten seconds later the anti-aircraft guns opened up. Blinded by the searchlights, swearing at the ineptitude of the gunners and searchlight crews, he lost the He 111.

A brilliant coruscation of shell bursts uncomfortably near sent him corkscrewing away in successful evasion.

Landing back at Middle Wallop, intending to grab the first soldier he saw and chop him into small pieces, he found that the time was past midnight and the Colours and Letters of the Day had changed since he took off. He had, therefore, flashed the wrong identification and the Germans had fired the right one: whether because German Intelligence was superbly accurate or by sheer fluke, who knows?

On 26th July the squadron moved to Gravesend, a former civilian airfield on the south bank of the Thames, near its mouth. Here, they were in the Biggin Hill Sector, with Squadrons Nos. 32, 600 and 610. The officers lived in the control tower. The sergeants slept on camp beds in an empty house just inside the barbed wire fence that had been run round the aerodrome, and ate their meals in a hut behind one of the hangars. In this hangar was the De Havilland Comet in which Scott and Black had won the Mildenhall to Melbourne air race.

Also on the airfield was a small factory making fuel tanks for Spitfires. The factory hands were soon subjected to a lucrative form of leg-pulling by the sergeant pilots. As soon as an air raid warning was given, the civilians used to drop their work and very sensibly run to the air raid shelters, while 501 Squadron was scrambling. By the time the squadron landed, the workers would be emerging from shelter. This was the appropriate moment for one sergeant pilot to call loudly to another: 'How did you get on?' And, whether his friend had seen the enemy or not, back would come the reply: 'Oh, not too badly. I got a 109 and a Do 17. What about you?' 'Not as well as you. I only got a He 111.' To all of which the civilians would listen with grateful admiration.

In consequence, when the bold sergeants appeared in the local pubs that evening they were almost drowned in free beer.

The war in the air was putting increasing pressure on Fighter Command: on 27th July, Lacey flew six times, and three times on the next day.

The most noticeable effect of these strenuous days was the ever-present fatigue. There was always some physical strain in flying a fighter, but this was small compared with the mental effort. At all times the fighter pilot had to keep his reactions razor sharp. When he was simultaneously holding his position accurately in a formation and scanning the sky for the enemy, his whole nervous system protested under the burden. Already the fighter pilots of the RAF were doing more work in one day than mind and body could reasonably support over a whole week. Day after day they flung themselves on to the ground or into a deck chair, when they landed from a patrol, and fell instantly into heavy sleep until the harsh voice of the Tannoy ordered them to scramble again.

Photographs of Lacey taken during the Battle of France and the Battle of Britain shew a smooth-faced boy who looks eighteen and not the twenty-three that he was. They also shew that he wore his forage cap at what must have been the most rakish angle in the Service: only his right ear seems to keep it on his head at all. Spikes of corn-coloured hair, undefeated by the brush, remind one of a schoolboy's unruly thatch. Compared with the more rugged aspect of his contemporaries he hardly appears old enough to entrust with an expensive aircraft, let alone capable of leading a section in combat and shooting down the enemy with ferocious accuracy.

The war, despite the ravaging weeks in France and the tiring weeks at Middle Wallop, despite the eroding effect of reaction to incessant flying, always-lurking danger and the frequent death of friends and comrades, was still very much a game to the fighter boys. A game in which you had time to play practical jokes at the expense of gullible civilians (who would have laughed even more loudly than you, if they had been admitted to the jest); a game in which you spent the daylight hours with your heart thudding in fearful anticipation of the next scramble; a game in which you reverted every evening after stand-down to the normal life of young men like yourself in peacetime: an evening at the flicks or a dance, with some of the boys or one of your girl friends, or over pints of beer in the local.

At night, there was no difficulty in falling asleep. But sleep was too often restless, invaded by dreams of head-on collisions with Me 109s, of bullets hammering on the armour plate a few inches behind your head; of some friend whom you had seen going down in flames that afternoon – only a couple of hours before you were ordering a round of beers in the 'White Hart' or the 'Leather Bottle'.

Sometimes the game was seen to be a very dirty joke indeed. As when, on the day that the squadron moved to Gravesend, 'Pan' Cox was shot down – apparently by your own anti-aircraft batteries at Dover.

'Things were getting hectic.' Lacey remembers. His logbook

81

shows four patrols on the 27th July, and two flights from Gravesend to Hawkinge and back, amounting to almost four hours' flying in one day with six take-offs, six landings, and four belly-wrenching howls from the Tannoy to 'scramble, scramble, scramble'.

On the 29th July, operating from their forward base at Hawkinge, on the Kent coast, 501 were in action over Dover once more; and unhappily, with the opinion they had now formed of the gunners' aircraft recognition. Of a large force of Ju 87s and Me 109s, they shot down six and damaged four. Pilot Officer R. S. Don had to bale out and was taken to hospital. Bringing a damaged aircraft in to land, Pilot Officer E. G. Parkin overshot, injured himself, and another pilot was temporarily non-effective in hospital.

The pilot strength of the squadron at the end of July, was:

Squadron Leader H. A. V. Hogan, Flight Lieutenant G. E. B. Stoney, Pilot Officers P. R. Hairs, K. N. T. Lee, R. S. Don, E. G. Parkin, J. A. Gibson, K. R. Aldridge, A. J. Bland, R. C. Dafforn, B. L. Duckenfield, Midshipman L. Lennard, Flight Sergeants Morfill and Payne, Sergeants Howarth, Wilkinson, Lacey, MacKay and Farnes.
Pilot Officer F. T. Andrews was Adjutant, Pilot Officer J. C. Nixon, Intelligence Officer, and the Medical Officer was Flight Lieutenant D. A. Davies.

August began with a sluggishness which was, withal, ominous. The world knew that a tremendous German invasion of Britain must be imminent. The civil population wondered when, where and how terribly the first massive air raids would begin. They braced themselves to face paratroops and a seaborne force that might strike anywhere. Fighter Command, in its Staff offices, its Operations Rooms and its squadrons, nerved itself for the looming battle against crushing odds.

Yet the atmosphere of a game persisted. No. 501 Squadron patrolled daily from Gravesend and Hawkinge; while on the ground, the pilots' nerves were stretched taut by the anticipation of the shrill order to scramble that would come at any moment from the Tannoy loudspeakers; when the day's work was done and they were lined up in their best blue, along some congenial pub's bar, nothing seemed more unreal than German gunfire and the stench of an aircraft in flames. The RAF played cricket against the Fire Service at Lord's, and the rush to see an evening paper was as much concerned with seeing how the teams had done as with learning about the war situation.

Nothing can break the British spirit, and adversity only strengthens it; yet dismay is to be avoided, and it was therefore as well that the real danger in which the country lay was known to so few.

At the start of the Battle of Britain, the RAF serving at home could call on 1,250 fighter pilots and about 600 fighter aircraft. The total squadron strength of Fighter Command was 29 of Hurricanes and 19 of Spitfires. No. 11 Group, which covered south-east England and must therefore expect to carry the greatest burden, mustered 6 Spitfire Squadrons and 13 Hurricane squadrons.

Controlling and positioning the fighters from the ground was the duty of the Control and Reporting System, an organization in which radio, radar and the Royal Observer Corps were integrated.

Overall control was exercised from the Operations Room at HQ Fighter Command, where a table map showed the whole of the British Isles and the seas for forty miles around. On this table were vari-coloured arrows and symbols, shewing the position, direction of flight, strength and height of every single aircraft or formation which was airborne anywhere within the whole British area. On the walls were displayed details of the squadrons, with their available aircraft and pilots, throughout the Command; for purposes of reinforcement and tactics.

The four Groups of Fighter Command (No. 10 in the west, No. 11 in the south-east, No. 12 in the midlands and No. 13 in the north) each had a HQ Operations Room, which reported to that at Fighter Command, and shewed, on its map table, similar information but limited to its own area and small overlaps of its neighbouring Groups.

Within each Group there were Sectors, corresponding roughly to the main airfields; and it was from these Sector

Operations Rooms that the ground fighter controllers were in direct radio contact with the fighters.

Information about anticipated enemy movements in the air was first reported from radio listening posts which listened out for snatches of German radio-telephone conversations that would betray activity across the Channel. As soon as enemy aircraft were airborne, they became liable to detection by the radar stations around the British coast. The original chain of these was known as 'Chain, Home' or CH, and its stations could only pick up aircraft flying above a certain altitude and without accuracy in counting numbers or assessing range. Later, a different type of radar was introduced to supplement these, known as 'Chain, Home, Low': this equipment was able to follow aeroplanes down to lower altitudes and to obtain readings on range and numbers. Last of all came 'Chain, Home, Extra Low'; but with the increase in sensitivity there went the penalty of vulnerability to interference: the more accurate equipment was also more affected by cloud and other conditions.

Aircraft flying within sight of shore or overland were reported by Royal Observer Corps posts, whose staffs depended on phenomenal ability at aircraft recognition and a few simple means of computing heights and speeds.

All this reporting by radar and observers went straight to the Group Filter Rooms. Here, naturally, there was much duplication and multiplication of plots; brought about by several sources reporting the same formation. From the jumble of plots shown on the map tables, Filter Officers resolved a single plot for each raid (the term for all aircraft, whether single or in formation, whether friendly or hostile), using the best information from all that available. These filtered plots were then rapidly told through to Group and Sector Operations Rooms: mainly by exceedingly attractive WAAF plotters, who spent long spells with head-and-breast sets on, in watches of forty-eight hours on duty and twenty-four hours off, accurately passing vital information which, though it appeared in front of them as prosaic, impersonal letters and figures, affected men's lives and the safety of Christian civilization.

A Sector Operations Room was an annexe of a fighter

pilot's cockpit, an extension of his faculties, an extra pair of eyes and a sixth sense of intuition.

On the sunken floor stood a large-scale plotting table around which WAAF and airmen stood, wearing head-and-breast sets, receiving information from the Group Filter Room. With long rakes, like those of croupiers, they moved coloured arrows to show the progress of each raid. Alongside these were small stands on which were the identity, height and strength of the raid. Friendly fighters appeared with the prefix 'F' in red on a white ground. Hostiles with a bold, black 'H' on a minatory yellow.

On a balcony above the plotting floor were ranged four Deputy Controllers, usually NCOs, who, with a chart and a course-and-speed computer, could work out the track of any individual Hostile or Fighter and direct the pilot of the latter towards the former. On the main balcony a few feet higher sat the Controller. He would control fighters directly from the plots shown on the table or hand them over to one of his deputies. Beside him were an Army Searchlight Officer and an Anti-Aircraft Officer, who, on the Controller's orders, instructed their respective sites to illuminate or fire or remain inactive.

Messages were passed from ground to air in a simple code. 'Angels' meant height in thousands of feet – 'Angels fifteen', 15,000 ft – 'Vector' meant steer. Enemy aircraft were 'Bandits', and an order to land, refuel and rearm was simply 'Pancake'.

A close relationship quickly grew between fighter pilots and their controllers. All that the latter could do, in the early days, was to put their fighters up-sun and above the enemy, and to vector them to the best position in the shortest possible time. They also had to maintain a flow of information about the enemy, without being so long-winded that the pilots either forgot what they had been told or were left no time for the vital exchange of messages among themselves. A good controller made an essential contribution to a successful interception; a bad one could ruin the chances of the best of pilots.

Here, then, lay Britain's strength in those opening days of August 1940.

The RAF was faced by three German Air Fleets. In Denmark and Norway, Air Fleet No. 5 had 40 fighters (twin-engine), 130 bombers and 50 reconnaissance machines. In France, Belgium, Holland and northern Germany, Air Fleets Nos. 2 and 3 primed themselves for the main assault. 60 reconnaissance aeroplanes, 250 twin- and 800 single-engine fighters, and 1,450 bombers were operational and fully crewed, with ample men in reserve.

Only the vagaries of the British summer, with its sudden days of overcast, rain or haze, delayed the onslaught.

Chapter Seven

THE HEIGHT OF THE BATTLE

ON Thursday the 8th August 1940, it came.

Four hundred German aircraft operated over the south coast of England and along the English Channel; but most of the activity was well to the west, in the Sussex and Hampshire areas, and 501 Squadron was not called upon to join battle.

The weather in Kent and east Sussex was still bad. Sergeants Howarth and Wilkinson, landing together in bad visibility, collided and wrote off both their aircraft without, happily, injuring themselves.

Strange faces were beginning to appear on the squadron, too: Polish pilots, who had escaped by a variety of routes when their homeland was over-run, were coming to fortify the RAF. Flying Officer Witorzenc, and Pilot Officers Lukaszewicz, Zenker and Koztowski, were posted to 501.

It was not until the 12th August that the squadron played its part again in the main defence of the island.

At half-past eleven that morning, when airborne on their way to Hawkinge from Gravesend, the Controller at Biggin Hill called them sharply. 'Vector zero-eight-zero. Thirty bandits approaching Thames estuary.'

They had been cruising at economical speed, called 'Liner'.

The Squadron Commander snapped 'Buster' on the R/T and instantly, as they swung to port on an easterly heading, they increased to maximum cruising speed.

'Bandits at Angels four,' the Controller told them.

'Message received and understood.' The leader was curt, scanning the sky.

Occasionally the R/T crackled as a section leader chided one of his wing men for keeping bad formation; once or twice someone called out that he had spotted what looked like a formation dead ahead ... and then they all saw them.

'Nasty, wicked-looking little Ju 87s, diving absolutely vertically, trying to bomb a destroyer. The destroyer was putting up a magnificent show; doing everything except slow rolls.'

There was an escort of Me 109s, but the Hurricanes went straight for the Stukas. Lacey picked out one which was streaking eastward at sea level. The dryness in his mouth had gone, now that nervous anticipation had given place to the excitement of the chase. With his right flying boot hooked into the toe-strap of the rudder bar and his left beating its usual tattoo on the floor of the cockpit, he overtook his quarry and lined it up for a deflection shot from above and to the left. A three-second burst, and he broke to the right to come in again from that side. Another three-second burst, a spurt of flame-shot smoke, and a pillar of water foaming and creaming up as the dive bomber plunged beneath the sea.

Pulling the stick hard back he climbed furiously to 4,000 ft again and fastened his eyes on another Ju 87, which dropped its bombs in the estuary as soon as it saw him coming, and turned east. Throttling back, Lacey opened fire from 250 yards dead astern, while tracer from the rear guns hurtled past his wings and over his cockpit canopy. His mouth was dry again: that damned tracer, every sizzling streak of it looking as though it was going to pierce through his guts. He kept his thumb on the firing button, feeling the shuddering of his Hurricane as its eight Brownings hammered at the rear turret. Suddenly, the air ahead was clear: there was no more tracer; he had killed the rear gunner. He was within a hundred yards now, gaining. At fifty yards, the enemy was on the fringe of a bank of cloud and Lacey opened fire once more. The Ju 87 flick rolled to the left, out of control, with a dense plume of black smoke spouting from its engine. Then he lost sight of it and as he did not see it hit the water or the ground he could only claim it as a probable.

At 12.40 the squadron scrambled from Gravesend to the Manston and Ramsgate district, where they found 30 Me 110 Jaguars and 20 Me 109s at 5,000 ft.

Lacey slanted down from the starboard quarter, on to a Me 110, starting to shoot at 250 yards and continuing till he was out of ammunition. White smoke belched from both engines and he saw the pilot bale out.

Two Me 109s were on his tail, he had no ammunition left, so he opened the taps and plunged into a big cloud and stayed there till he was out of harm's way.

Flying Officer Lukaszewicz was killed in this action.

Landing, eating a hasty lunch of bully beef sandwiches and strong tea, out at the dispersal point, he flung himself into a canvas chair and was just falling asleep when one of the other NCO pilots shook his shoulder.

'Hey! Ginger.'

'Whaddayouwan'? Go'way ...'

'There's a visiting Air Marshal around the place.'

'I'll stand up when he gets around here – if I'm awake.'

'It's the Inspector General, Air Chief Marshal Sir Ludlow Hewitt.'

'Well, he can take my place on the next scramble, if he likes. God! I'm tired.'

'Look out: here he comes ...'

There were other visitors at that instant also. The air raid sirens wailed just as a formation of He 111s and Ju 88s swept over. The bombs burst deafeningly around the aerodrome, and 'The IG, although so much older than we were, was just as nippy at diving down slit trenches!'

But despite the bodily and mental tiredness, there was a party after the squadron's return to Gravesend: Sergeant Pilot J. H. Lacey was gazetted that day as having been awarded a Distinguished Flying Medal.

Familiarity with combat, and confirmation of a man's prowess in it, however, did not lessen the strain of aerial warfare. Indeed, for some, the longer they survived the greater seemed the probability that their turn to be killed could not possibly be much more deferred. Whatever the reason, there were many by now who reacted agonizingly to every announcement from the Tannoy: and Lacey was one of them. Every time the loudspeaker hummed its preliminary note on being switched on, he had to rush from his bed in the dispersal hut, or from the grass under his Hurricane's wing, where he was lying, and vomit. Whether the message turned out to be 'AC Plonk to report to the Orderly Room immediately', 'The film in the Station Cinema tonight is ...', or the anticipated '501 Squadron – scramble!' the effect was the same. His stomach muscles jerked convulsively, his fatigue-sodden body and mind could not control them, and he must be sick.

On the 15th August they came to readiness at ten minutes past four in the morning and Lacey flew six times before the day was done. On one scramble, flying as Red Three, when the squadron encountered more than twenty Do 17s between Maidstone and Rochester, he attacked the No. 3 in the rear section with a four-second burst, but found himself closing too fast and broke hard to the right. He saw his incendiary bullets going into the wings, but before he could continue this engagement a second Hurricane had taken on the bomber and he looked for another. He saw about thirty more Dorniers, flying east, and attacked one from 250 yards astern, with a nine-second burst. He saw it nose sharply down in a forty-five-degree dive with smoke enveloping it and disappear in a cloud. With the remainder of his ammunition he attacked a third Do 17, inconclusively. The squadron destroyed or damaged 14 Ju 87s, for the loss of two Hurricanes whose pilots baled out, and damage to one.

In two more actions that day, 501 accounted for eight more enemy aeroplanes damaged or destroyed.

On the 16th, the squadron was ordered off to find 20 Dornier 17s, 6 Me 109s and 10 Me 110s, in the Hastings-Dungeness area. Lacey, who was in Red Section, found after they had climbed through a thick layer of cloud, that the three aircraft had become separated from the rest. He took over as rear guard, zig-zagging behind the other two.

Red Leader, on the R/T, gave 'Tallyho!' and dived at a Do 17, and immediately five Me 109s dived on Red Leader. Lacey went to his defence, closed to within fifty yards of the leading Messerschmitt, and gave it a three-second burst. The German fighter whipped into a vertical dive, with black smoke rippling from its cockpit and engine, into the clouds.

Day after day, his log-book tells the same story. To Hawkinge in the morning. Patrol ... scramble to intercept ... patrol a convoy ... scramble again ... back to Gravesend.

On the 18th the squadron was in a fight over Canterbury, during the morning, in which two pilots were wounded, one killed and another suffered burns. In the afternoon they were scrambled to the protection of Biggin Hill, which was under attack.

At 4.50 PM, seven Hurricanes, on their way back to Hawkinge after having landed at Gravesend following this last battle, met fifty mixed bombers and fighters. They shot down two Me 110s, but Flight Lieutenant Stoney lost his life.

At the end of the day's fighting, Red Section were put on Night Readiness.

On the 24th, Lacey flew eight times. Action began with a dogfight with thirty Dorniers and Me 109s, at 10.30 AM, four miles north-west of Dover, from which P/O Zenker did not return. Lacey, flying Number Two, saw his leader attack one of the bombers, whereupon No. 3 in the last section broke right. Lacey attacked it head-on, from below, and saw it go into a dive with smoke coming out of an engine; then a Me 109 opened fire on him and he had to abandon the bomber to deal with it.

At 1 PM the dreaded Tannoy sounded off again, scrambling the squadron to the Ramsgate area. They found fifty Ju 88s, with a strong fighter escort. Lacey saw that one of the 88s had just started its dive, so he got on its tail and opened fire as it pulled up at 4,000 ft. He could see his incendiaries smacking into both engines and the rear turret; tracer was coming back at him from the upper rear gunner, but this stopped at the same time that the starboard engine went dead, its propeller wind-milling to a halt, and the port engine began to make smoke. Lacey turned aside to avoid a collision and the lower rear gunner fired at him; he turned and attacked again, from dead astern; and, so as to avoid the lower gunner's fire, from slightly above. A few seconds after his final burst he saw the pilot take to his parachute while the bomber dived into the sea near the Goodwins.

On the fourth flight of the day, attacking a mixed force of Do 17s, Do 215s, and Me 109s, he had just put a burst into a Do 215, when there was a streak of vivid colour across his bows, a clang from somewhere in the Hurricane's nose, and he felt the aircraft pitch forward and down as its engine cut. Looking down and finding that he was right above Lympne aerodrome, he glided down with a dead engine, to find on landing that he had a bullet through the radiator. While fitters and riggers were patching his aircraft, he went to the Mess for a quick meal; by the time he had eaten, the aircraft was fit to fly back to Gravesend.

Flying six and eight times a day, never less than four times, week in and week out, had brought all the pilots to such a state of tiredness that they could not bother even to walk away from their aircraft on landing. In that blisteringly hot summer it was easiest just to lie on the grass in the shade of a Hurricane's or Spitfire's wing and fall instantly asleep. If the Intelligence Officer came to ask you for a combat report you put one in, and with it your claims for aircraft destroyed or damaged. If nobody asked you, you did not trouble to volunteer the information; until, perhaps, the day was finished and memory dulled. In this way, many of the pilots were never credited with victories they had won. Time and again there was another scramble before an IO could make out combat reports on the mission just completed, and by the time the boys were back from that one, everyone had forgotten about the previous sortie ... and so on, with scrambles piling up and each obliterating the details of its predecessor. Time after time, a pilot who had scored successes on an early sortie must have been killed on a later one before ever being able to make a report which would, at least, have given him permanent credit for what he had done.

Not that the Battle of Britain pilots needed any sordid accretion of numbers after their names to proclaim their skill, bravery and stamina. Just by being airborne, reacting to each

German raid, they were saving the world: their presence was enough, on many occasions, to turn the enemy away before combat was joined. And the strain of operational flying was no less when no enemy was encountered, than when a vicious dog-fight was being decided: for each time they flew they expected to see the German and attack him, and it was this as much as, perhaps more than, the moments of battle, that frayed their nerves and robbed them of refreshing sleep and proper relaxation.

Some of them became so emotionally numb that they were like automata; morose, withdrawn, wanting neither food nor companionship; dragging themselves through each day in almost a stupor. Others, more highly strung, teetered constantly on the brink of frenzy: talking incessantly, smoking heavily, forcing themselves to loud laughter and feigned high spirits. But among the unfriendly silence on the one hand and the horseplay on the other, were the majority: level-headed, thoroughly professional, in control of themselves. Perhaps Lacey's laconic Yorkshire character was as much responsible for keeping him sane and alive through that period, as his naturally brilliant eyesight and swift mental and physical reaction to quickly-changing events. If it hadn't been for that damned, whining Tannoy, he would probably never have shown any outward signs of nervous wear. Each day made the situation more desperate, with an average loss of fifteen fighter aircraft and ten pilots, nearly all in 11 Group.

Neither memory nor official records reveal details of the next few days. Log book entries tell of several hours' flying, but no combat, until we come to the 29th, when, in what his log-book calls 'a spasmodic engagement with Me 109s in the Dover area', Lacey added another of these enemy fighters to his score.

On the next morning, over the North Foreland, he fought an engagement with thirty or forty Me 110 Jaguars which did not stay to dispute the issue: he put two long bursts into one of them, saw it stagger into the low haze with smoke emerging from one engine, and reckoned that he had a 'probable' at least. There was a twenty-minute break at base, while the aircraft were refuelled and rearmed; but the German Air Force was under orders to batter its way through the British defences and prepare the ground for Hitler's final, devastating assault: 501 was soon in the air again, this time with the Controller ordering: 'Vector two-seven-zero. A hundred-plus Bandits approaching Dungeness.' And how right he was, for there were the He 111s and Me 110s in a countless swarm.

Lacey, Yellow Two, picked the 110 which was leading a big formation and attacked from ahead, opening fire at 400 yards and continuing until, as his combat report describes his actions: 'Collision was imminent. So I broke underneath and when I pulled up I saw that the Me 110 had left the formation and was going east with smoke coming from its port engine. Climbing, I found a He 111 just ahead, also going east, rather slowly, as though it had been damaged. I attacked, opened fire at 250 yards, and saw the undercarriage drop and the port engine catch fire. As I closed, long flames and thick black smoke made vision difficult. I had to break off, as I was attacked by several 110s. I continued fighting until I had no ammunition left.'

But there was more in store before the 30th August came to a close. Lacey recalls that 'Later on that day I had an interesting experience.' It seems that a news reel film unit was working on Gravesend aerodrome and wanted a picture of a squadron scramble. Agreeably, the CO allowed his pilots to get into their cockpits, while the cameras whirred, preparatory to demonstrating a quick, dummy, take-off.

But even in those circumstances they had their R/T sets switched on, and with the cameras barely in position, the Sector Controller's voice dinned in the pilots' ears: 'Scramble. Bandits in Thames estuary.'

The delighted cameramen marvelled at the co-operation they were receiving: the Hurricanes thundered across the airfield, climbed steeply, formed up and headed eastward.

Over the estuary, 501 saw well over fifty He 111s, with several Do 17s and a big escort of Me 109s, flying due west. The CO led them into a head-on attack and they held their squadron formation, four vics of three, in the manner of heads-on of that day. 'On the CO's word we all put our fingers on the trigger; not looking where we were shooting, but just keeping our formation and flying straight through the middle of the Germans. With ninety-six machine-guns blazing straight at them, it must have been pretty frightening. It had the desired effect and the Heinkels split all over the sky. We were then able to pick them out one at a time. This time, however, as we were going in, I started to be hit by very accurate fire. I could see bullets entering my wings, coming in from directly ahead, and also straight into the engine.'

Oil sprayed all over the cockpit, from the punctured oil cooler at the bottom of the radiator. He pulled out to starboard, and as he banked, bullets were piercing his wings from beneath. He completed his turn and began gliding southward, away from the battle. Immediately, bullets hammered through his aircraft from the rear. 'So whoever was doing the shooting was either very lucky or knew a lot about deflection, because it had been constantly changing.'

He jettisoned his oil-smeared cockpit hood and 'was about to bale out when I suddenly realized that I was going to fall in the Thames; and I wasn't particularly keen on that.'

It was a heart-stopping moment. The air was full of hostile fighters and his speed was very slow now that he had no engine. If he did bale out, the odds were that some sporting Luftwaffe pilot would shoot at him as he hung beneath his parachute. Either way, he was a sitting duck. He could only hope that other Hurricanes and Spitfires were holding the attention of the enemy enough to divert them from pursuing aircraft which were already out of the fight.

The engine was showing no signs of catching fire, and the oil had run dry and was no longer spurting all over him, so he decided to stay in his machine, glide as far as the Isle of Sheppey, and bale out there. But when he arrived over this small piece of land he saw how unlikely it was that, without knowing the wind direction, he would succeed in landing on it. So he made for the mainland, aware by now that he had enough altitude to glide all the way back to Gravesend.

Pumping the undercarriage and flaps down by hand, he circled the aerodrome to lose height and made a perfectly judged landing. 'And finished my run, with a dead engine, right smack beside the point from which I'd taken off. Much to the joy of the news reel unit, who were busy taking pictures of my landing.'

There were eighty-seven bullet entry holes in Lacey's Hurricane, and innumerable bigger gashes where lumps of metal, ripped internally from the aircraft, had been smashed right through it.

'I was awfully pleased with myself, having brought the aircraft back in that condition; until I eventually saw the Engineer Officer. His remark was, "Why the hell didn't you bale out? If you'd baled out of that thing, I'd have got a new aircraft tomorrow morning! Now, I've got to set to work and mend it."

Lacey's postscript is: 'It certainly made me change my ideas about what was a good thing and what was a bad thing.'

On the last day of August, he killed his eleventh confirmed victim. To add to this were three probables and two damaged.

Action came at 3 PM. 'Scramble zero-three-zero. Bandits attacking Hornchurch.'

Hornchurch was a major aerodrome to the north-east of London, vital for the defence of the capital. When the seven serviceable Hurricanes of 501 Squadron got there, they were surrounded by thirty Do 17s and twenty-four Me 109s. Lacey, as Red Leader, headed the rearguard section. He saw a dozen Me 109s lance into a stern attack and called a warning to the squadron leader. The Hurricanes reefed tightly round to face the Messerschmitts head-on and the enemy split to port and starboard as they blasted through them.

Lacey took his eyes off the 109 in front, flashing past his right flank, and glanced in his mirror: there was another of the swine on his tail, diving with its guns winking red-yellow splashes and sending glittering arcs of tracer within inches of his head.

He throttled back sharply and the enemy overshot, diving steeply. He put his nose down and went after it. It twisted to left and right, but he turned with it, awaiting his chance. The Me pilot showed no imagination: regular turns to port and starboard alternately; as soon as Lacey had established the pattern of his evasive tactics, he put himself in position for what must inevitably happen. At the split second that the target next jinked, he thumbed his firing button. The acrid cordite smoke in his cockpit was as heady as incense to a religious devotee, as he watched his bullets smash into the 109's fuselage and stitch a long row of gaping holes along it. The Me steepened its dive. So did the Hurricane. With the aircraft vibrating and his controls stiff, Lacey put in another long, well-aimed burst. A gout of vivid flame, a streamer of grey smoke laced with oily black, and the German fighter hurtled on, plainly out of control with its pilot dead or crippled.

A few seconds later, when Lacey eased out of his dive, he saw a brilliant flash of flame followed by a great pillar of smoke as the Me 109 plunged into a petrol storage tank on the estuary shore.

501 Squadron entered September 1940 with a pilot strength of: Squadron Leader H. A. V. Hogan, Flight Lieutenants J. A. A. Gibson and A. R. Putt, Pilot Officers S. Skalski, P. R. Hairs, R. C. Dafforn and B. L. Duckenfield; with three in hospital, K. R. Aldridge, K. N. T. Lee and F. Kozlowski. Flight Sergeant Morfill, and Sergeants MacKay, Lacey, Wilkinson, Loverseed, Farnes, Howarth, Adams, Glowacki, Whitehouse, Gent and Henning.

On the sunny Sunday which opened the month, they tangled with twenty-seven 110s, 16,000 ft above Tunbridge Wells and damaged one.

Monday began with an air raid, at 7.50 AM, during which bombs fell on the edge of the airfield. It was a day of frequent scrambles and wild dog-fights that sprawled all over the sky, splitting formations so that pilots often found themselves alone among a vastly greater number of the enemy. Since the days in France, when 'Cobber' Kain had declared, half-seriously, 'We have decided, in future, not to take on odds of more than four to one!' the RAF had been pitted against numbers gravely superior to their own. Four to one, five to one, even eight to one, were routine. But on the first Monday in September 1940, completing exactly one year since the declaration of war, one pilot of 501 reported finding himself tackling fifteen Do 17s, and another, also alone, nine He 113s.

It was bad enough for the Laceys, the Morfills and the

Instructor to the Yorkshire Aeroplane Club. Lacey (*right*) with a joy-riding Moth, June 1939

First flying course for RAFVR pupil sergeant pilots, Perth, 1937. Lacey is third from the left, middle row; Hawkeye Lee, fourth from left, back row

◄

Sergeant J. H. Lacey, September 1939

501 County of Glouceste[r] Squadron in France, Ma[y] 1940. *First row, left to right* J. H. Lacey, 'Jammy' Payne[,] Paul Farnes, Morfill, Donald McKay, Bob Dafforn; *middle row:* Hawkeye Lee, 'Hairy' Hairs; *back row:* Dicky Huls[e] (killed), F/O Pickup, Adj. and unknown pilot

▼

. H. Lacey with mother and Nicky after receiving his commission as pilot officer, January 1941

Lacey on the wing of his Spitfire wearing the parachute and scarf presented by workers in the Australian parachute factory, July 1941

▲ Sqdn. Ldr. J. H. Lacey (*centre*), P/O R. B. Connell (*right*), and P/O F. Irvine (*left*) in front of a Spitfire, February 1945. Operating in Central Burma, they shot down three Japanese aircraft in twenty-four hours

▼ 'Jimmie Nutti', the seven-year-old Gurkha boy, found starving and ill with malaria in Calcutta and adopted by No. 17 Squadron then flying over the Burma Front

MacKays, who had been continuously in action for four months; but it scarcely offered a hope to the novice. That morning, a young pilot officer, A. T. Rose-Price, was posted to the squadron. That afternoon, he was killed in action over Dungeness.

For Lacey, it was a day of confused memory. First they were vectored eastward, then west, then south; told to make Angels twenty, then ten, then back up to twenty-five. Now he was turning tightly on the tail of a Me 109 at twenty-two thousand feet, a few minutes later he was spinning from eighteen thousand to six thousand, striving to shake off the four 109s which seemed glued to his slipstream. Not long after, he was scudding over the wavetops pumping bullets into a Heinkel, then breaking off with scarcely enough room in which to manoeuvre as a pair of Mes came hurtling at him from his starboard quarter.

At ten minutes past eight in the morning, he was leading Yellow Section of 'A' Flight when the squadron waded into fifty Me 109s which were escorting about as many Do 215s, near Ashford.

'Yellow Leader to Yellow Section. Climbing to attack those three 109s above the main formation.'

Numbers One and Two, craning their necks, could discern what their leader's sharp eyes had first observed: three Me 109s climbing fast to get high enough to attack the Hurricanes from astern.

The R/T was bristling with the usual crisp warnings, interspersed with the Controller's orders and information.

'Behind you, Red Two . . .'

'Break left, Blue Three, break left . . .'

'Can you see him, Green Leader?'

'I'll take the one on the extreme left, Red Section . . .'

Lacey's section attacked the three top-cover 109s before they were able to launch their own attack. He took the leader for himself: its red-painted cowling rather asked for trouble. As they dived in line astern, he put nine seconds' worth of ammunition into the fuselage and wings, taking his thumb from the trigger when the target banked out of his line of fire. Breaking steeply with it, he endeavoured to line up his guns for another burst but held his fire when he saw the hood whip open and the pilot plunge out.

All the other 109s were engaged, as there was another British squadron in the area by then, so he set his sights on a Do 215 at the rear of the formation. Glancing down, he saw that the pilot of the Messerschmitt had done a delayed drop and opened his parachute five thousand feet below.

He fired at the Do 215's starboard engine and almost at once it turned to the right with smoke feathering out from the nacelle. He fired again, but his ammunition ran out and he last saw the bomber making its way slowly across the sea, losing height.

In the afternoon, over Dungeness, with his stomach still raw from the retching effect of the Tannoy's '501 Squadron scramble!' he led Yellow Section into an armada of 30 He 111s, 30 Do 214s, 20 Ju 88s, and 30 Me 109s and 110s.

At 300 yards he began with a three-second shot at a Me 109 which was leading a vic of five. It produced a dramatic result: the enemy fighter exploded with a violence that swept its companions aside, turning one of them upside down. Lacey felt his Hurricane bucketing in the churning air, and he instinctively shut his eyes as he swept into the ball of smoke which eddied around the explosion. A hail of metal from the shattered aircraft rattled against his wings and canopy and for a moment he thought that he was under fire.

Bursting out of the smoke he heeled over to tear into an attack on the remaining four with Yellow Two and Three holding their positions on either side of him. The sky was strewn with darting, feinting, lunging fighters, and with bombers which clumsily tried to evade the Spitfires and Hurricanes that could spare a few seconds from the Messerschmitts. Somewhere in this tangle, Yellow Section used all their ammunition without being able to make any more certain claims.

The war had been in progress for a year, and Fighter Command had brought down 1,776 German aeroplanes. Flying sorties of about only an hour's duration, fighter pilots had covered 17,000,000 miles: of these, 4,500,000 were flown in August 1940.

The pattern of the times is inexorable and appears to be never-ending. Rise at an early hour: 4 AM, perhaps, certainly

98

never later than 6.30. Fly standing patrol somewhere around 'Hell's Corner', the south-east angle of England. Land at Hawkinge. Scramble ... scramble ... and scramble again. One more standing patrol, waiting for an enemy who might or might not come. Back to Gravesend. Maybe, a night stand-by. If not, a hurried visit to some place where there are ordinary people to mix with and take one's mind off revs and boost and deflection shots. Finally, a flop into bed and instant sleep, with always the semi-conscious appreciation that tomorrow might be one's last day of life. Or the day after that. Some time next week at the latest, surely, with the huge enemy formations coming and coming again, and the odds seldom better than five to one.

And still there is room for humour. The growing number of Poles, Czechs, Norwegians, Dutch, Belgians and Frenchmen appearing on RAF stations, gives rise to new problems and birth to new anecdotes. A favourite one is about the Polish airman who, on being told by a Station Commander that he is to be remanded for a Court Martial, drops instantly in a dead faint. It is only when the interpreter explains that, at home, this usually means execution by a firing squad within four hours, that the CO understands why it is that he cannot strike similar terror into the hearts of his British airmen. There is another, too, about the foreign nobleman, commanding a unit of his countrymen, who had to be dissuaded from his feudal method of dispensing justice: arguing against the necessity to hear evidence when a man is on a charge, he declares 'If *I* say he is guilty, he *is* guilty'. The RAF likes those stories.

The 5th September. '501 Squadron scramble!'

The familiar voice of the Controller. 'I've got some trade for you coming in from the south. Maintain Vector one-zero-zero, making Angels twenty-five.'

And the CO, matter-of-fact, sounding even indifferent. 'Understood. Any idea how many Bandits?'

'Looks like sixty-plus.'

'Good show.'

A few seconds' pause, then some wit breaks R/T silence with a terrifyingly realistic imitation of machine-gun fire, in the best music hall style.

But you can't hide your identity from men with whom you share almost every waking second. The Boss, sounding reluctantly amused, tells him to shut up.

The Controller again. 'What Angels now?'

'Just passing through Angels twenty-two.'

'OK. Level out. Trade approaching from south at Angels eighteen.'

'Understood.'

'I'm going to turn you, presently, and bring you in from up-sun.'

'Thanks!' The irony in the leader's acknowledgement is not entirely accidental.

'Bandits three-o'clock, range forty. Start turning now on to two-seven-zero.'

The squadron wheel, turning to their right so that they will face the enemy who is approaching from the south. They settle down to a due westerly heading, and the Controller's voice gives them some more help. 'Bandits now ten-o'clock, range fifteen.'

They begin to wriggle on their parachute packs, feeling the chafing of their harness straps as sweat starts involuntarily to run over their backs and chests. In their silk gloves, palms grow moist, while mouths feel dry and eyes burn with the concentration of staring, staring, always staring ... at the man ahead and the man on your wing ... at the burning, sunlit sky ...

'Target should be eleven-o'clock, range five ...'

And instantly the leader's exultant 'I've got 'em ... Tally-ho! Tallyho!' And the tight wheel, with your heart pounding and your eyes smarting with the glare on those threatening cross-shapes which are suddenly Messerschmitts and Dorniers and Heinkels in countless numbers. The air around you boils and seethes as you are tossed around and sucked down by slipstream and explosion. Here a bomber goes to smithereens in a mighty thunderclap that almost shatters your perspex windscreen, as incendiary bullets hit its bomb bays. There a fighter in an inverted, flaming spin – God! You see it is a Hurricane and recognize the letters on its side ... so much for your double date that evening to take those two girls to a dance ...

one of them would have to find another partner … and now there are three 109s on your tail and you are on the tail of one yourself. Who would get whom first?

Grip the stick, thumb poised over firing button. Ease the throttle back a shade … one … two … three … four seconds – would the brute never show signs of damage? Ah! That is better: a puff of smoke … another two seconds … a flicker of crimson along the edge of his cowling … then, suddenly, the 109 is on its back and a sprawling figure is dropping from its open cockpit.

Look in the mirror, throttle back, watch the three behind overshoot, open the taps again, get the rearmost in your sights … one, two, three seconds … a vomit of oil-streaked smoke, the Me staggers, a sliver of metal drums against your cowling … you see a wingtip sawn off as you give another burst … and the pilot doesn't get away from that one.

One hour and forty-five minutes later, you land back from the longest operational sortie you have flown to date, but with two more Me 109s confirmed to bring your score up to fifteen.

On the 6th, there is more fighting, in which Sergeants Adams and Houghton are killed.

On the 7th you do an air test, and go on leave.

'I had a special reason for wanting to go home on leave to Wetherby then. I had not told my mother that I had been given a DFM and I wanted to be at home when it was published in the Press.'

It was a laudably filial consideration, but the maternal reception, as he was greeted at the door of 15 Fairfield Villas, was hardly what he had expected.

Ginger is not the tallest of men, but his mother's eye-level was about that of the flying badge on his left breast.

'What are you wearing that ribbon for, Jim?'

Might as well make a joke of it … 'I thought it would be a good idea: get me more drinks in the local pubs!'

'Well,' he was told firmly, 'you're not going out with that stitched on you. Take it down immediately.' So he stayed at home that evening.

'Of course the next day the announcement was in the newspapers; and then I was in trouble again: because I didn't want her to worry about the fact that I had ever been in any danger.

On the day that he went on leave, his squadron took part in an interception of the biggest formation of enemy bombers yet to be seen in this war: four waves of them, each numbering a hundred, with strong fighter escort. For an hour and a half they pounded the London docks, leaving them in flames whose glare could be seen in the evening sky, five hours later, from twenty miles away. The RAF, for the loss of twenty-two aircraft and thirteen pilots, brought down over a hundred hostiles.

A week's leave didn't take long to get through. Perhaps the best part of it was being able to sleep late every morning and to eat good meals at his leisure.

When he rejoined the squadron, on the 13th September, they were at Kenley, thirteen miles south of London and four from Croydon, where they had been posted on the 10th.

The move was popular with the squadron. They were delighted to find that 'The station was populated by WAAF. Talk about high life! At least, after having been the only squadron at Gravesend, with a very small Station Headquarters, and pretty much in the wilds there, *we* thought it was.'

A fifty-minute patrol yielded nothing, and then the weather deteriorated.

But it wasn't long before Ops. were on the telephone to the crew room to ask for a volunteer to take off and look for a Heinkel which was somewhere over London. 'But,' they warned, 'owing to the unbroken cloud everywhere in the southeast, whoever goes will probably be unable to land: it will mean baling out.'

Lacey said he had always wondered what it was like to bale out, and off he went.

It was a long stalk, and he was airborne for two hours.

The Controller guided him eastward, at 14,000 feet, above the solid layer of cloud that covered the whole of the south-east of England. A turn to the south, another to the east; a turn to the south-east, then east again. The Controller's directions were concise and intelligent, but the Heinkel was elusive. Until . . .

'I saw it, slipping through the cloud tops, half in and half out of cloud, making for the coast. I didn't know where I was, because I hadn't seen the ground since taking off. I dived down on him and got in one quick burst which killed his rear gunner. I knew he was dead, because I could see him lying over the edge of the rear cockpit. Of course the Heinkel dived into cloud, and as I was coming up behind him I throttled hard back and dropped into formation on him, in cloud. He turned, in cloud, two or three times, still making a generally south-easterly direction, and I'm quite certain he thought he had lost me or that I'd stayed above the cloud. Actually, I was slightly below and to one side. You couldn't see very well, in cloud, through the front windscreen of a Hurricane, but you could see through the side quarter-panel and I was staying just close enough to keep him in sight through this. I stayed with him in all his turns. He made one complete circle and then carried on south-easterly. Eventually he eased his way up to the top and broke cloud, presumably to see if the fighter was still hanging around. Just as he broke cloud and I was dropping back into a position where I could open fire, the dead gunner was pulled away from his guns and another member of the crew opened up on me, at a range of, literally, feet.

'I remember a gaping hole appearing in the bottom of the cockpit. The entire radiator had been shot away, and I knew it was just a matter of time before the engine would seize, so I put my finger on the trigger and kept it there until my guns stopped firing. By that time he had both his engines on fire and I was blazing quite merrily too. I think it was a glycol fire rather than an oil fire, but *what* was burning didn't particularly interest me: I knew that *I* was burning and I was going to have to get out.

'As soon as the guns ran out of ammunition, by which time the He 111 was diving steeply through the cloud, I left the aircraft.

'I came out of cloud in time to see my aircraft dive into the ground and explode. While drifting down, I saw various people running across the fields to where it had crashed. There was one man passing almost underneath me, when I was about five hundred feet up, so I shouted. This chap stopped and looked in all directions, so I shouted again, "Right above you." He looked up, and I saw that he was a Home Guard.

'As he saw me, he raised a double-barrelled shotgun to his shoulder and took aim. I knew it was a double-barrelled shotgun, because I was looking down the barrels; and they looked like twin railway tunnels!

'I shouted, "For God's sake don't shoot," and amplified it with a lot of Anglo-Saxon words that I happened to know, and continued to exhort him not to shoot for the rest of my way down; and added a lot more Anglo-Saxon words.

'Eventually I fell in a field and just sat there, but he still kept me covered with his gun. I said "Hang on a minute, while I get at my pocket and show you my identity card." He put his gun down and said, "I don't want to see your identity card: anyone who can swear like that couldn't possibly be German."

'I was a little bit singed (his trousers were burned off to the knees) but had beaten out the fire on the way down, and my face was a bit burnt. Not very burnt, because I was always careful to pull my goggles down as soon as I saw an enemy aircraft. I'd seen too many of my friends in hospital who hadn't pulled their goggles down, and burnt eyes were a pilots' trademark that I was determined not to get.'

He had come down near Leeds Castle, which was the Officer's annexe of the Shorncliffe Military Hospital. Here he had an argument with a doctor who wanted to put him to bed; Lacey was determined that he would first telephone the airfield and inform the squadron that he was safe. But, owing to the bombing, there were so many telephone lines down that he had to abandon it after two hours of trying.

'So I told them that they must send me back, and I had to get back before the squadron packed up for the day, otherwise a "Missing, believed killed" telegram would go off to my mother, and I didn't want her to have that kind of shock.'

The doctor had told him to report sick on returning to camp, so he dismissed the ambulance at the Guard Room and walked to the Officers' Mess to report to his CO. By then, he had on a new pair of trousers which concealed the burns on his legs. 'So I was able to go straight back on readiness.'

It was only now that he learned that the Heinkel he had just shot down had bombed Buckingham Palace.

His log-book carries the entry 'Must remember to leave bombers alone in future. They are shooting me down much too often.'

He didn't fly on the following day, because he was drawing new uniform and flying equipment.

Which brought him to the 15th September 1940: the day on which the climax of the Battle of Britain came, and the date that is celebrated every year as Battle of Britain Day.

This was the crucial day, on which Hitler staked everything to overpower Britain. Great Britain, never truly more great.

It was half-past eleven in the morning when, on that Sunday of glorious sunshine, 250 hostiles, stepped from 15,000 to 26,000 feet, crossed the coast between Dungeness and Ramsgate. Five squadrons from Nos. 10 and 12 Groups, and sixteen from No. 11, were ordered off to fight them. 501 Squadron was in action by noon, against twenty Do 17s and fifty fighters, near Ramsgate. They shot down an Me 109, damaged another and lost a Dutch pilot, Pilot Officer Van der Hove Esterrych.

The second attack came in the afternoon. Twenty-one squadrons in all were again used. No. 501 joined battle over Heathfield, at 2 PM.

Lacey, flying Red Three, said in his combat report that they intercepted a raid flying north-west at 16,000 feet. They attacked from slightly below, head-on, throttling back to 150 mph so that the approaching speed would not be too great. He opened fire, himself, at 400 yards, pulling his Hurricane's nose up as his target approached until he went over the vertical and stalled into a right-hand spin. By the time he had regained control and climbed to 17,000 feet there were no other aircraft in sight.

'Red Three to Red Leader. Where are you?'

'Red Leader to Three. Just north of Brighton.'

'OK. I'll join you. What Angels?'

'Angels fifteen.'

'OK. Be with you in a minute.'

But twelve yellow-nosed Messerschmitts (the vaunted Abbeville wing) had other ideas.

In a flash, Lacey found himself racing head-on towards them. He dipped his nose as though about to dive under them, then pulled back the stick and rocketted up in a loop, to attack the last one in the formation, which was lagging. He put a satisfactory burst into it while still inverted, and as he had plenty of speed, half-rolled off the top of his loop and followed the formation. 'Who didn't seem to have seen that their last man was diving vertically with flames pouring back over his cockpit hood.'

Closing to 250 yards, he fired on No. 3 in the rear section. It pulled out of position with a white stream of glycol leaking out of its radiator.

Around him were shell-bursts from the anti-aircraft guns, and he hoped that they would not hit him. But there was no time to worry about friendly ground gunners, for the remaining ten Me 109s were charging at him. He fired the last of his bullets into the leader and dived vertically into cloud.

He has two comments to make on this event which are worth recording. 'After the squadron had been split up, and I was trying to rejoin, I was, as usual, showing a lot more interest in where I'd been than in where I was going: because the danger always came from behind; I kept looking over my shoulder, to make certain there was nothing coming in behind *me*. As I brought my head round from one shoulder to look over the other I saw that I was doing what amounted to a head-on attack on twelve yellow-nosed 109s. My immediate reaction was to push the stick forward and dive to hell out of it.' But he didn't.

And, after he had destroyed one and severely damaged another, and was being set on by their ten companions: 'The others were thoroughly annoyed about the whole business and this time I did have to dive out of it.'

The third hostile wave of the day was at the coast soon after 7 PM, by which time the defending fighter pilots were weary to the marrow, their eyes dulled, their reactions hazy. In the twilight, with the air over three counties filled with aircraft, it was not easy to tell foe from friend or to avoid flying into the fire of someone else's combat.

Personal memory and official records are alike blurred and

incomplete. Somewhere, sometime, in the course of that evening's fighting – there was yet a fourth, and final, attempt to destroy England, at about 8 PM – Sergeant Lacey shot down two more of the enemy: a Me 109 and a He 111.

On the 16th September there was a blessed day of inactivity: the English summer, playing its familiar tricks, produced high winds and heavy rain, which kept aircraft on the ground.

On the 17th, after the squadron had been scattered in a dogfight and were ordered to rendezvous over Maidstone . . .

'I was flying back over the Dover area towards Maidstone and, looking down, saw 5,000 feet below me, fifteen Me 109s. I was probably well and truly over-confident by this time, having attacked twelve of them a couple of days before and got away with it. As I had been told to rendezvous at 15,000 feet and was now at above 20,000, I thought that as I had to lose some height I might as well dive through these people and have a crack at them on the way down.

'Building up speed rapidly in my dive, I found, of course, that the controls were growing very stiff. Well before I was within range, the 109s obviously saw me and did what was the most stupid thing they could possibly have done: stuck their noses down and started to dive in the same direction. Theoretically, that should have given me a non-deflection shot, but I must have been travelling 100 mph faster than they were by this time and I never got a shot at them at all. I hurtled straight through the formation; which left me in rather an embarrassing position – sitting in front of fifteen 109s.

'Everything in the world seemed to hit me. I completely lost control of the aircraft and realized that I'd had it.

'I jettisoned the hood and as I pulled the pin out of my straps I was, literally, sucked out of the cockpit without having to make any effort to climb out: I was going so fast that there was a tremendous difference between the low pressure in my cockpit and the high pressure of the wind rushing past outside.

'Everything went black. I thought for one horrible moment that I'd gone blind. And then, for an even more horrible moment, that I must be dead. But (and his voice begins to shake with laughter as he is telling this) as I automatically put my hand up to my eyes, I found that, as we had no self-disconnecting oxygen tube in those days, my tube, before it broke as I was dragged out of the aeroplane, had pulled my helmet down over my face!

'I wasn't blind in the least little bit,' he explains, 'all that was wrong was that my eyes were in my helmet!'

'I pushed it back on to my head and I could then see why I'd lost control of the aircraft: the whole of the tail unit had been shot off. It was spinning down flat, and slowly, in front of me. The 109s were taking turns to come in and fire at it, passing very close to me. I didn't want to pull the rip-cord, in case this attracted attention. When I took off, the clouds were at 5,000 feet, which was quite enough for a parachute to open comfortably, so I decided to fall into cloud before opening mine.

'I was spinning end-over-end, and this was starting to make me feel sick, so I straightened myself out and this stopped my somersaulting. I now began to fall, quite comfortably, head-on, at an angle of about sixty degrees to the vertical. Although I must have been doing about 140 mph, there seemed to be no tendency for my eyes to water. I was quite observant and self-critical and there was no sign of becoming unconscious in free fall. I put my right hand across my body to grasp the rip-cord, which was on the left, and found my arm acting like a small aerofoil: it started me revolving. It was easy to control the turns of my body by moving my arms. By this time the cloud was quite close and the 109s seemed to have disappeared, but I did not pull the rip-cord until I was in cloud. And, as guaranteed by the makers, the parachute opened perfectly comfortably. I came down in a field.'

Once again, he was very close to Leeds Castle.

No sooner was he taken to this hospital than 'I got a rocket from the doctor who had seen me there only three days previously.' And who, of course, thought he must be in hospital having treatment for his burns.

Once again there was the immediate insistence on putting him to bed and his retort that he must telephone base first. And again, after two hours' unsuccessful attempt to get in touch with Kenley, the sergeant pilot was put in an ambulance and dispatched to his squadron.

It took them rather longer to get back, this time, because the driver was a pretty FANY who accepted his pleas that they must stop frequently for him to fortify himself, at numerous pubs, with brandy.

'So we got back rather late.'

There was an institution, in those days, at Kenley: a small, good-looking, and warm-hearted WAAF corporal cook, Jean Campbell. Though of much the same age as the sergeant pilots, she took their daily dangers to heart as though they were her sons. Nothing she could do for their comfort was enough, in her view; and when one was missing she would stay up all night, if necessary, to welcome him back with a cup of tea. It is some measure of what this gentle creature suffered, and of the devil that sat on the shoulders of fighter pilots at that dark time, to record that, during four particular days at Kenley, the three other beds in the room where Lacey slept each had two different occupants.

When his FANY with a taste for brandy that matched his own deposited him at the Mess, Corporal Jean gave him a royal welcome. And brewed a fresh pot of tea.

The Germans changed their tactics, the directions of their raids altered, the daylight effort lessened a trifle in favour of night bombing. For a few days, the squadron flew without excitement.

On the 27th September, Lacey was flying No. 2 in Yellow Section when Do 17s and Me 109s came along from the south, at 18,000 feet.

Before the squadron could attack the Dorniers, the Messer-schmitts dived protectively in front. Lacey was instantly caught up in a dog-fight with five Me 109s, which was presently joined by the rest of his section. In the melee they lost height rapidly until they were at 7,000 feet. At fifty yards he hammered a two-second full-deflection shot into a 109 which immediately went into a vertical dive in which one wing was wrenched off. He saw it crash in a field, and its wing hit the ground 200 yards away.

September wore to a quiet close, with only one more combat,

when he chased a Ju 88, on the 30th, and after firing from 300 yards, closing to fifty, he saw glycol escape from its starboard engine which presently stopped a few seconds before he lost the 88 in cloud.

At the end of the month, the squadron was still commanded by Squadron Leader Hogan, with Flight Lieutenant E. Holden, DFC, and Flying Officer D. A. Jones as Flight Commanders; and Flying Officers N. J. M. Barry, V. R. Snell and E. B. Rogers; Pilot Officers K. W. Mackenzie, P. R. Hairs, K. N. T. Lee, R. C. Dafforn, Witorzenc; Flight Sergeant P. Morfill; Sergeants P. P. C. Farnes, J. H. Lacey, DFM, R. Gent, Whitehouse, Patterson, Pickering, C. J. Saward, R. W. E. Jarratt, S. A. Fenemore. Non-effective in hospital, were: Flight-Lieutenant J. A. Gibson, DFC, Pilot Officers K. R. Aldridge, Kozlowski, Skalski; Sergeants A. Glowacki, W. B. Henn, Crabtree, W. Green, D. N. E. Mackay.

And Sergeant Pilot J. H. Lacey, DFM, had just been awarded a bar to his decoration.

In the sixty-one days of August and September, Fighter Command lost 298 pilots and 615 aircraft.

With October came a marked falling off in the enemy's fly-in effort. Now, there were only hostile fighter sweeps to cope with over south-east England by day.

On the 5th October, Squadron Leader Hogan and Flight Lieutenant Holden each got a 109 and Pilot Officer Mackenzie damaged a third.

On the 7th Lacey claimed a Me 109 probably destroyed, when he shot its port aileron off, at 23,000 feet, followed it as it went down, firing short bursts at it, and watched it dive vertically into cloud, streaming glycol.

His next confirmed success fell on the 12th. The squadron took on 30 Me 109s which were returning to France. Lacey followed his down to the sea, shooting at it intermittently, until it made a pancake landing in the Channel, when he reported that the pilot had climbed out and was swimming around strongly.

But enemy activity was still persistent, for Lacey flew four times that day.

On the 15th, in a tussle 21,000 feet over the Isle of Sheppey, he was shot at by a Hurricane: but whether this was a mistake in identity by the other pilot, or whether there was a captured Hurricane among the Germans, nobody knew.

On the 25th, the squadron lost Pilot Officer Goth, who had only been with them a week, when he collided in mid-air with Pilot Officer Mackenzie, DFC.

On the 26th, after running into fifteen Me 109s ten miles north of Beachy Head, at 29,000 feet, Lacey found all the enemy engaged before he could choose one and had to descend to 14,000 feet before he was able to open fire on the rear machine in a pair just above cloud. It caught fire at once and fell into cloud with its rear fuselage burning fiercely. He then fought its partner until all his ammunition was expended; when, his combat report says, he 'found it expedient to dive into cloud and escape.'

There was one more fight in store for him before the Battle of Britain drew to a close. In a last, typically frenzied dog-fight that wove condensation trails over fifty square miles of sky, that swayed and see-sawed between fifteen and twenty-five thousand feet, he shot down an Me 109 and damaged another.

So October closed and the Battle of Britain ended, and Sergeant Lacey's eighteen enemy aircraft destroyed in that battle was the highest score among all the pilots of Fighter Command. To add to these were four probables and six damaged, and, in France, five more destroyed.

November and December were occupied with daily patrols and never a smell of the enemy, until, on 17th December, the squadron returned to Filton. Squadron Leader Hogan had been promoted to wing commander and posted, and Squadron Leader Holden, DFC, was in command, with Flight Lieutenants E. V. Morello and D. Jones as his Flight Commanders.

Lacey's last clear recollection of 1940 is of Christmas afternoon.

'After a delicious Christmas lunch, the CO said, "Right ... I'll teach you so-and-so's to drink too much at lunch time. We'll do a battle climb."' And so they did: as his log-book records, 'to 30,000 frozen feet'.

Chapter Eight

THE BLITZ

On 15th January, 1941, 740042, Sergeant Lacey, J. H., became Pilot Officer J. H. Lacey, (60321).

On the last day of his service as an NCO, the Officer Commanding No. 501 Squadron entered this endorsement in his flying log-book: 'This pilot is credited with twenty-three victories in air combat and his flying ability is well above the average.'

The official list of British air aces of Fighter Command, up to 31st January 1941, puts Lacey at the head. In addition to his twenty-three confirmed, he had four probables and six damaged to his credit. Among the other fighter pilots with high scores were:

P/O E. S. Lock, DSO, DFC and bar, 22 at least.

Sgt H. J. M. Hallowes, DFM and bar (reported missing), 21.

S/L A. A. McKellar, DSO, DFC and bar (killed), 20.

S/L A. G. Malan, DSO, DFC and bar, 18 and 6 probables.

S/L R. R. Stanford Tuck, DSO, DFC and bar, 18 at least.

F/O H. Orton, D.F.C. and bar, 18.

P/O E. J. Kain, DFC (killed), 17.

And, lower down the list, two whose names were later to win great fame:

F/L A. C. Deere, DFC and bar, 11, probably 1 more, and assisted to destroy 2 others.

S/L D. R. S. Bader, DSO, DFC, 10, and damaged several more.

Until now, Lacey had not been interested in a Commission. There was little difference in status between officers and NCO pilots and life in a Sergeants' Mess was comfortable. But, he says, he remembered that holders of the DFM are entitled to a cash bounty of £20 on being discharged from the Service. In order to become an officer, he would, on paper, have to be formally discharged as an airman and re-enter the RAF with his Commission. This, he claims, decided him: it was a quick way to get his hands on the bounty!

He went on a fortnight's leave, and his home town was waiting for him.

As the local newspaper put it: 'Wetherby paid a well-deserved tribute to one of its sons on Wednesday night, when, at an informal gathering in the Town Hall, a presentation was made to Flying Officer James Harry Lacey, DFM and bar.' (With understandable chauvinism, Wetherby promoted its distinguished son rather more rapidly than had the Air Ministry).

'Although the meeting was called at very short notice the Hall was full. Captain J. H. Hudson, MC, JP, presided and made the presentation – a silver tankard inscribed as follows: *Presented to Sergeant Pilot James Harry Lacey, DFM and bar, by the people of Wetherby, in recognition of his conspicuous skill and gallantry in defence of freedom. 1940.*'

Among the speeches was one by his old headmaster, who recalled that 'As a young boy at school James Lacey was shy and reserved. On one occasion he said to me, in the playground. "Please, teacher, these other boys and girls are following me and they are harassing me" – not a bad word for a boy of five.'

Manifestly, he displayed at an early age the independence that is his hallmark; although by the time the schoolmaster spoke in reminiscence, James had largely overcome his repugnance for being followed by girls.

The presentation from his fellow townsmen was an event which Ginger Lacey remembers with affection and pleasure.

Being out of the war for two weeks, at the period, was bearable.

Compared with the May to October months, there was little urgency in the squadron's affairs. To be among his family and old friends, to have Nicky, his smooth-haired terrier, constantly at heel, was a return to normality which he would have been glad to prolong.

He returned to the squadron to find that they were doing a lot of night flying, from Chalmy Down near Bath.

The German 'Blitz' had been directed, in the last few weeks, at many targets besides London and some of these were in the west: Cardiff, Bristol and Avonmouth, Plymouth, Swansea and Portsmouth. In the Midlands, within easy range of Filton and Chalmy Down, Coventry and Birmingham were major enemy targets. At night, the fires caused by Goering's bombs lit the sky for scores of miles, and the fighters on night flying duty could only go towards the stricken cities and hope to find the enemy. The Operations Rooms could give very little help.

It was frustrating to fly, with mounting anger and hatred, seeing the acres of flame by night and the aftermath of devastation by day, and be unable to strike back. The winter weather brought snow, fog and rain, so that the opportunities to operate were all too few: and when they did occur, the fighter pilots could even, on occasion, see enemy bombs falling past them from bombers overhead, ugly, black eggs in the glare of the towering flames below, without being able to see the raiders who were so close. And here was a new menace: what an end to a fighter pilot's life, to be killed in the air by a bomb.

Lacey was glad to get away from the hopeless business of chasing Germans through the night sky – like looking for a fly, in the dark, in the Albert Hall, someone described it – and go to London to be decorated with his DFM and bar. Paul Farnes had to go for his DFM, and they were summoned together.

Like all wartime ceremonial, there was more exuberance than solemnity about it, and 'after quite a convivial evening the night before, and one or two drinks in the morning to get rid of the hangover', the two alumni of 501 Squadron presented themselves at the royal residence. They were, they agreed, 'most impressed by Buckingham Palace'; which, bearing in mind their habit of understatement, was praise which the architect might well have liked in writing, to frame, had he been alive. 'But Farnes,' Lacey tells us, 'was not particularly impressed by an Admiral who was marshalling us. He persisted in trying to do up Farnes's top button.' This, in the eyes of a highly operational fighter boy of the period, was the ultimate in gaucherie. The unfastened top button, traditional since the Great War, was the recognized means of distinguishing between Fighter Pilots and the rest – those bomber, coastal, training, army co-operation and transport types one believed existed somewhere. 'Farnes resisted strenuously,' we are told; and imagination quakes at what must have been the very senior Naval Officer's reaction to being wrestled by a non-commissioned officer of the junior service – the only one, of course, in which such insubordination could conceivably be encountered. 'He told the Admiral that he might be very good with a battleboat, but he knew nothing about fighter pilots.' But Sergeant Farnes's intentions were of the best, and he was correctly buttoned when he appeared before King George VI.

Lacey does not feel that he acquitted himself as well as he might have on his only visit to the Palace.

The procedure – and he was confident of his ability to carry it out – demanded a smart march up to His Majesty. A smart left turn to face him. A bow. A pace forward to receive your medal. Answer any questions the King might put to you. A pace back. A smart right turn. And march off.

Pilot Officer Lacey was wearing crêpe-soled shoes and the carpet had a pile an inch and a half thick. 'I turned rather smartly to the left, but my feet stayed where they were. Eventually' – eventually! – 'I had to shuffle them round. Then I was quite baffled when the King asked me when I was awarded the DFM, I couldn't remember. And to make it even worse, he said "And when were you awarded the bar to it?" and I couldn't remember that either. I think by the time I left he was convinced that I was an imposter, collecting it for someone else.'

There was something of a party that evening. There always was, after an investiture, which brought old friends together from all over the country. Lacey, when he woke next morning, couldn't remember leaving the 'Chez Moi', a Soho club much favoured by air crews. Looking around, from the sofa on which he had slept, he found that he was still there.

And so back to Filton and Chalmy Down, and the long spells of inactivity caused by bad weather; the only variety, on one of the days when he could fly, provided by a barrage balloon which had broken free from the Bristol defences, that he had to shoot down.

Convoy patrols ... training replacement pilots ... formation flying. The weeks passed and life was unbelievably tranquil after the hectic weeks in France and at Gravesend and Kenley. On 9th April the squadron was posted to Colerne, on the outskirts of Bath.

And on the 17th they flew their first sweep over enemy territory, escorting eighteen Blenheims which bombed the docks at Cherbourg. Life seemed to have a purpose and reality again. At last they were taking the offensive, for the first time since being thrown out of France ten months before. It was odd, with memory so clear of that damnable Tannoy screeching its infernal 'Scramble', actually to be enjoying this. Where were those Me 109s? Why didn't they come and take a crack? We'd like to see them again. Look out! That flak was pretty close ... and the Blenheim boys are getting a hot reception ... takes nerve to hold steady on a bombing run, straight and level, presenting a good target to the ground gunners ... can't sit around here, watching ... here comes some more flak – quick! bank hard to port and climb a bit, to fox the Hun ... How easy it was to slip back into the old habits of self-preservation that were instinctive now, and would never be forgotten.

Only one day stands out in memory. Squadron Leader Holden and Pilot Officer Lacey were selected for the privilege of going to nearby Colerne to be presented to Her Majesty Queen Mary, the Queen Mother. Her Majesty's superb bearing and ineffable charm left an abiding impression on a man not readily impressed.

And then another week of convoy patrols, wing formation, squadron formation ... anything to pass the time until there was a real job to tackle once more ...

Until one morning the Squadron Adjutant came into the crew room. 'Anybody here flown Spitfires?'

'Why?'

'We've got to collect some for the squadron, from Exeter.'

Pilot Officer Lacey, who was bored, looked up from the 'Tee Emm' he was reading. 'Yes, I've flown Spits.' He hadn't, but he supposed they were no more difficult to fly than Hurricanes.

Twenty minutes later, he found himself in a Blenheim bound for Exeter; flown by a wing commander, no less: Charles Beamish, Colerne's Wing Commander Flying.

'There you are, Lacey,' said the wing commander, as they circled the aerodrome, 'all lined up, waiting for you. Look good, don't they?'

'Yes, sir,' replied the bold pilot officer, trying to sound keen. Where the hell was everybody? There had better be at least one pilot around the place to tell him how to handle the damn things . . .

'Find them much different from a Hurricane, to fly?' Oh! These chatty wingcos.

'N-n-no . . . n-not really, sir . . .' It looked as though 88 Squadron had flown away in their brand new Spitfire IIs, and left their old Spit Is for 501 to pick up without a pilot to do the honours and hand them over formally.

They had.

Wing Commander Beamish decided he'd like to stretch his legs. 'I'll walk over with you and see you take off.'

'D-don't trouble, sir . . .'

'No trouble, old boy . . .'

Old Boy! He'll change his tune when I wrap the squadron's first Spitfire round the Flying Control Tower. Inspiration! 'I think the Flying Control chap wants you, sir . . . yes . . . he's beckoning you from the window . . .'

'Oh, is he? Suppose I'd better go and have a word with him . . . tell him I'll be taking off again in a few minutes . . .'

Lacey chased after a passing airman in overalls, who looked as though he must be a flight mechanic. 'Airman! Know anything about Spitfires?'

'What d'you want to know, sir?'

'Quick – into the cockpit and show me how to start the engine . . . where all the knobs and taps are.'

The airman pushed his forage cap back and scratched his head, eyeing Lacey's pilot's wings and DFM ribbon with its rosette.

By the time the Wing Commander Flying arrived alongside, Lacey was just waving away the chocks, with confidence.

Once he was airborne, trial and error provided the identity of the various levers which the airman had lacked time to explain. He delighted in the lightness and responsiveness of this aeroplane, compared with the old Hurricane.

In the next three or four days he ferried most of the Spitfires to Colerne and was able to make sure that he was allotted the best of them as his own aircraft. So, when Wing Commander Flying came and invited him to do some cine practice (simulated combat with camera guns to record results), he thought it would be interesting to palm him off with the worst of them; a sluggish machine with a lamentable rate of climb, a radius of turn that would have been fatal in action and a derisory top speed.

Beamish acted first as target. Lacey promptly positioned himself on his tail and stayed there, despite frenzied evasive action, until he had used all his film. Now it was Lacey's turn to be the target. 'Right,' said the wing commander. 'Begin evasive action.' Whereupon Lacey whirled round and sat on his opponent's tail once more. It took Wing Commander Beamish a long time to expose his film.

They landed, Lacey wondering what would happen now. 'I can't believe I'm as bad as all that,' Beamish told him. 'We'll change machines and go up again.' This time, Lacey could neither get on to his opponent's tail nor shake him off his own.

Coming in to land, Lacey noticed that the 'T' outside the Control Tower, which showed the wind direction, had been turned 180 degrees. On both their take-offs and on their first landing, the wind had been blowing from due west and they had, of course, taken off and landed into it. He duly made his approach in the reverse, and now correct, direction. Touching down, letting his tail drop, he could not see ahead because the up-thrust nose of a Spitfire obscured its pilot's view. Half-way along the runway he was hurled forward in his straps with a violence that threatened to rip them apart; his head jerked forward with a snap that nearly tore it from his shoulders. There was a deafening clang of rending metal, his windscreen and canopy shivered into a myriad cracks, his engine screamed and died. With his intestines feeling like cold jelly, he fumbled with his straps, found his hands trembling, and heard the siren and bell of a fire-engine and an ambulance approaching. Wing Commander Flying had collided with him, head-on.

'Needless to say, I was fireproof.'

In May the squadron became operational on Spitfires. On 17th June it flew another sweep; but, as back area escort, didn't cross the French coast.

On 24th June, Lacey was promoted to Flight Lieutenant and now commanded 'A' Flight, which he had joined as a sergeant one year and nine months previously.

The new Squadron Commander was Squadron Leader A. H. Boyd, DFC and bar, who had accumulated a score of twelve hostiles with Nos. 65 and 145 Squadrons. 'B' Flight was commanded by Flight Lieutenant R. C. Dafforn, DFC, who had been a sergeant with Lacey in France.

On the next day 501 was posted to Chilbolton, in Hampshire, a grass airfield which had no domestic accommodation. This station was a satellite of Middle Wallop, which was now commanded by Group Captain (later Air Chief Marshal) Sir W. Elliot, DFC. 'A' Flight Commander found himself a billet in a house called 'Testcombe', on the river Test, owned by a Mrs Disraeli. He admits that he was very comfortable there.

Now began a period of night flying patrols over Portsmouth. With three or four aircraft airborne at the same time, stepped at two thousand-foot intervals, pilots were ordered to stick rigidly to their allotted level. One night, Lacey was flying at the top of the stack when he saw, silhouetted on the background of a fire in the docks and the searchlight beams, a Ju 88. Instantly, determined not to let slip the opportunity for which everyone on the squadron had waited seven months, to bring down their first hostile aircraft by night, he slipped into the familiar mood of intense concentration; his left foot impatiently rat-tatting on the cockpit floor, his thumb on the firing button; his throat constricting and his teeth chewing involuntarily on his lower lip.

The hunt was on. The bomber circled lazily, no doubt admiring the effects of its night's work. Cagily, Lacey brought his Spitfire round until he was a hundred feet above and to one beam. Then he depressed his nose, pressed home the trigger and exulted as he saw the bright splashes of his de Wild ammunition along the enemy's fuselage.

The Ju 88 dived, and Lacey, forgetting his orders to stay within his fixed height band, followed it.

His eyes were dazzled by the strong light from below, exaggerated by the surrounding blackness. For an instant he lost his quarry; found it and touched off a short squirt; saw it flit away and disappear momentarily; saw it reappear and fired again.

Two or three thousand feet slipped by while he kept losing and finding it again; and now the Ju 88's turns became tighter and faster; until it was holding its own with the Spitfire, baffling Lacey.

The R/T came to life, and he heard the voice of the CO, who was supposed to be flying at the level immediately beneath him, report that he was in contact with the enemy. Then ...

'A thought crossed my mind ...'

Lacey called the CO. 'Please flash your navigation lights.' And, as he had suspected, the aircraft which he was trying so hard to shoot down blinked out a series of bright flashes.

Not all the perils of flying, especially at night, were attributable to the Germans.

He had to lean heavily on Adrian Boyd's sense of humour when he met him in the crew room an hour later.

On 10th July, 501 gave high cover to twelve Blenheims bombing Cherbourg. Lacey, flying left weaver, called a warning that two Me 109s were diving to the attack. He broke, delivered a three-second quarter attack on one of them, and it dived into the sea in flames. Boyd damaged the other. There was no further interference with the mission.

There was another trip to Cherbourg that week, and this time he damaged a 109.

Exactly a week from then he was part of an escort for some Blenheims which were making an air-sea rescue search ten miles south of Portland, when there was a flicker of colour in the corner of his left eye and he turned his head sharply to see tracer fire licking past his port wing tip. He half-rolled and pulled through to find a He 59 marked with the red cross in his sights at a range of 250 yards, from which he let it have a two-second squirt. Closing to fifty yards, on its tail, he gave it another two seconds' worth of treatment and, as it was merely flying at 100 feet, it ploughed into the water and sank.

The red cross was no protection to aircraft which carried machine-guns and, indeed, initiated attacks. As long as twelve months before this time, two He 59s with red crosses had been forced down: their log-books showed that they were carrying out reconnaissance and reporting back by radio. The British Government thereupon issued a formal warning to the Germans that such aircraft would, in future, be attacked. Several of them had been shot down before Lacey got his and he was right not to hesitate in taking the action that he did.

It was while he was at Chilbolton that the factory in Australia which manufactured the first parachute to be made in that country, sent it to him as a gift; and with it, a silk scarf embroidered with the names of a hundred girl employees, some of whom had taken part in the production of both articles. These were a tribute to his success in shooting down the Heinkel which had bombed Buckingham Palace. The presentation was made by Air Vice Marshal Sir C. J. Quintin Brand, KBE, DSO, MC, Air Officer Commanding No. 10 Group; who, himself, had destroyed a Gotha in the last raid on England in 1918.

Next came preparation for a task which was to provide Lacey with the worst scare of his career.

Equipped with Spitfire IIs carrying thirty-gallon long range tanks under their port wings, the squadron carried out daily practices at 20,000 feet. Their object: to give high cover to bombers on an attack on the German pocket battleships Scharnhorst and Gneisenau in Brest Harbour.

On 24th July, 1941, they flew to Predannack, in Cornwall, the most westerly of fighter aerodromes, to refuel. At 2.42 PM they were on their way.

This was not a popular job. Flying a single-engined aeroplane over 150 miles of water never is. Brest was ferociously defended by one of the strongest flak belts in Europe. There was a big German Air Force fighter airfield nearby. And the tanks under the Spitfires' wing-tips made them unmanoeuvrable, particularly in turns to port, which became dolorously slow.

Five miles west of Brest, Flight Lieutenant Lacey, in the position of top weaver, saw two condensation trails overhead, shadowing the British formation, and climbed to investigate. Meanwhile, heavy flak had started to burst around him. Before he went up, he saw two bombers hit: one dissolved in a giant puff-ball of fragments and the other dropped vertically with flames and thousands of feet of smoke laying a pall behind it.

Urging the best speed from his machine, keeping his eyes on the two con. trails, he climbed to 30,000 feet before, from a thousand feet above, two Me 109s dived in a synchronized attack. Splitting as they came, one rushed at him from the right while the other swept round to settle on his tail. Desperately he turned into the man on his beam, reviling the tank that hung from his wing and dragged him back. A stream of tracer coruscated past. The 109 to his right flicked momentarily into his sights, he gave it a sharp burst, and the man behind loomed horribly in his mirror.

From the latter's gun ports burst vermilion jets of flame and bullets thudded into the armour behind Lacey's head.

With his senses on the verge of a black-out he held grimly to his dizzy turn, keeping one of his opponents intermittently in his sights and shooting whenever he could. For long minutes they churned round in a deadlock, neither able to get on the other's tail and Lacey unable to break because he would instantly have abandoned the only safeguard he had. This way, at least he could contain one of them: but it couldn't go on for ever; he hadn't the fuel to spare for one thing, if he wanted to reach Predannack again.

Like aerial dervishes, Spitfire and Messerschmitts clung to each other, and Lacey, snap shooting, at last heard the hiss of compressed air and felt the cessation of his gun's recoil that told him he had used the last of his ammunition.

If he was to live now, it must be a matter of airmanship, not marksmanship.

And the second Messerschmitt, having pulled away to one side, was making a deflection attack from abeam.

He tried to compress his body into the smallest possible space as tracer thrashed at him from the starboard side ... and then from port ... and from starboard again ... then from port once more ...

His legs and arms were stiff and cramped, his head was fogging as blood drained from his brain.

Once more the loose 109 pulled away, and this time it came in with terrifying accuracy.

In a last effort, Lacey pulled the stick back and sent his Spitfire leaping up in a near-vertical climb.

Two seconds later a tremendous blast of disturbed air pummelled him between the shoulders, a noise like the crack of doom battered at his ears; and in his mirror he saw the two Me 109s collide, hang in the air locked together, then swiftly begin to fall in a rapidly increasing spin; inseparably welded by the force of their collision at a closing speed of 800 mph, they sent off a shower of sparks that presently turned to flames; he saw one of the pilots bale out, but the other, who was flown into, must have been smashed to pulp.

He searched the sky and found himself alone. It was time to set course for base.

Half-way across the Channel he overtook a Wellington that was returning from Brest. It looked like a flying bird cage, its geodetic framework exposed by the fabric which had been shot away.

He came alongside to fly in formation with the bomber until they sighted home. The Wimpey pilot made delighted thumbs-up gestures, grateful for the fighter escort.

'Little did he know that I was hanging around there because I thought *he* might have some ammunition left for his guns and could escort *me* home.'

It was a fitting end to two years with 501 Squadron.

On the 18th August, 1941, he was posted as an instructor to No. 57 Operational Training Unit, at Hawarden, in Flintshire.

Chapter Nine

ON REST – BACK ON OPS

FOR a moment Lacey wondered whether he had forsaken the Royal Air Force in favour of la vie diplomatique. Saying goodbye, one morning, to the last surviving descendant of Benjamin Disraeli, he found himself, the same afternoon, settling down in Hawarden Castle, the temporary Officers' Mess, which was owned by Lord Gladstone. He had come a long way since a scattering of WAAF at Kenley had tasted like High Life.

1,620 hours of flying, more than half of it in the Service, and over 300 of those hours on operations, had left their mark on him. When he went to Fifty-Seven OTU he no longer looked the boy whose appearance belied his lethal accomplishments. The exuberance of fair hair was hidden with some austerity under an officer's Service Dress cap, his features had sharpened and there were lines about his eyes and cheeks. The diffidence apparent in his demeanour a year or two earlier had given place to a self-assurance which was evident even in formal group photographs.

Instructing on an OTU was described, not without euphemism, as 'a rest'; as though the inherent strain of flying, especially in company with inexperienced companions prone to error, could ever be removed entirely. Even so, there is no doubt that this pilot was, by then, in need of whatever could be offered in the way of resting.

'Hawarden,' he says bleakly, 'was not very interesting. Students came through on a production belt.'

But he remembers one exception: the Canadian 'Screwball' Beurling, who won renown in Malta and soon became legendary the world over as a sort of aerial Daniel Boone: an unkempt, rebellious individualist with fantastic gifts of marksmanship and timing.

Beurling first came to the new instructor's notice when he had finished his dual instruction on Miles Masters.

'I didn't give very much dual instruction: I'd been paid for doing that in peacetime, but in wartime I didn't think that the extra risk warranted it!' So much for Lacey's opinion of the average pupil's reliability.

The first time he led Screwball on formation training, the latter was flying Number Three, on his left. They practised gentle turns, tight formation, steeper turns, and ended with a dive over the airfield. Lacey had briefed the two pupils to break away and make individual landings after pulling out. Approaching in a shallow dive, building up a lot of speed, they crossed the airfield and he waved them away to carry out their landings. Then he went up in a steep, climbing slow roll. It was only when he was on his back that he realized that Beurling was still with him, tucked tightly in on his port; he stayed there till the roll was completed and Lacey had to call him on the R/T and order him down, or he would have remained in formation for the landing. 'There are no two ways about it, he was a wonderful pilot; and an even better shot.'

This, the Germans and Screwball Beurling's friends in Malta learned, when he used to pick his victim and nominate his shot at prodigious ranges and with unerring certainty. 'Guess I'll hit this one in the starboard engine' ... a burst from his guns ... smoke from the enemy's starboard engine. 'I'll get the pilot, this time' ... a few seconds' shooting ... and an apparently undamaged aircraft, free of smoke or flame, diving out of control with a dead man in its cockpit. Beurling was killed while landing at Istres long after the war was over.

The six months at Harwarden passed, for Lacey, very slowly. But they were made more tolerable when he realized that other pilots had their rough moments in this war, too. At least the risks he took were on operations, and the sooner he got back to them the happier he would be. But others never had the satisfaction of flying against the enemy, yet had to face situations which he would not have relished.

Such as his old friend, the former Chief Flying Instructor at the Yorkshire Aeroplane Club, Captain Worral, who had been

Sir Alan Cobham's navigator in the latter's flight round Africa in the Short 'Singapore' in 1927–8.

Aged about fifty-seven when the war broke out, he immediately joined Avro's as a test pilot. Lacey went to lunch with him one day in 1942, and just as he arrived Worral was about to test a Manchester. 'Sorry I can't take you up in this one, Ginger, but I've got a lot of boffins and flight engineers aboard. However, I've got another one to test before lunch, so I'll take you up with me in that.'

Half-way down the runway, when it was too late to stop, one engine caught fire. Worral took off, went round the aerodrome in flames, and landed.

'He strolled back and said, "Come on, Ginger, we'll go and test the other one now." As you can imagine, you couldn't have got me into that second one with an armed escort.'

He watched Worral take off again. Half-way down the runway, one engine of this Manchester also caught fire. The pilot flew round the circuit, in flames, and landed.

'This is a dear old gentleman of fifty-nine or sixty; and not even batting an eyelid: we went straight off to lunch as though nothing had happened.'

An OTU didn't seem too bad, in contrast.

In March, 1942, he got his wish and was posted back to a squadron. The Commanding Officer of the OTU, Group Captain D. F. W. Atcherley (later Air Vice Marshal, CBE, DSO, DFC), who was killed in 1954 when he was flying a Meteor over the Mediterranean, was sorry to see him go.

He wrote:

10th March 1942

Dear Ginger,

I was so sorry to have missed you yesterday as I would particularly have liked to have said goodbye and thank you to you before you went.

I got back in the Master just after you had left. However, as I missed the opportunity I am writing to wish you luck – I know you have got it, and to thank you very sincerely for the admirable job you have done here.

You may, or may not have guessed it, I don't know, but it was apparent to me from the word 'go' that your Flight was the best in the OTU. You have not only turned out good pupils, but you have also turned out good Instructors, and it was evident too that it was a happy concern from top to bottom. Well you have left your mark, and we will see to it that the standard is kept. I am not very hopeful of securing any official commendation for you, and anyway it is not a thing to discuss, nevertheless I would like you to know that if it lies within my power you shall have some recognition.

All of us wish you luck and are certain of the successes in front of you. You can reflect, if the subject interests you, on the probability or otherwise of having done more good for the general cause by your work here, than hundreds of others have; even in sweeps. At least that is what I think.

Cheerio,
Yours sincerely,
David Atcherley.

He joined No. 602 (City of Glasgow) Squadron, at Kenley. It was commanded by Squadron Leader B. E. ('Paddy') Finucane, DSO, DFC, an Irishman, who was at the time the subject of great notoriety for his swift accumulation of successes which had come after the Battle of Britain; and was later killed when his score stood at thirty-two confirmed.

This squadron was equipped with Spitfire 5Bs, which carried four machine guns and 20 mm cannons.

Lacey liked his CO and liked his aeroplane, and was beginning to enjoy life again.

On 24th March, exactly a fortnight after joining 602, he was in action for the first time since his rest. He took off in the afternoon as leader of Yellow Section, on a 'Circus' to Comines, with the rest of the squadron. They were at 25,000 feet near Cassel, at 4 PM, on their way to Comines.

The R/T buzzed in their ears as someone switched on to transmit.

'Yellow One from Yellow Two. My engine keeps cutting.'

'I wondered why you were keeping such lousy formation. OK turn back: we'll escort you.'

The squadron leader cut in. 'Red Three (who was his own left wing man) detach and join Yellow Section.'

'Understood.' Red Three sounded brassed off at having to leave before the party had really started.

Yellow Section peeled off with Red Three flying cross-overs behind them, diving for the coast, which they crossed at 7,000 ft over Mardyck. That was all right: no enemy fighters had interfered and they were well on their way.

A couple of minutes later, in mid-Channel, Flight Lieutenant Lacey counted his chickens. Something odd ... he counted again ... they had won a bonus: instead of five aircraft, there were six. The sixth was at the rear of the section and slightly below, climbing to catch up.

Lacey decided to take a closer look at the straggler. 'Yellow Section, I'm just turning back to have a look at that chap behind.'

The others flew on while he banked steeply away.

He ran at the stranger head-on and when they were four hundred yards apart it pulled hard round to port.

He recognized it as a Focke-Wulf 190.

If the Me 109 had brought a chill to him, the first time he saw it, the FW 190 was enough to make anyone pass blue lights.

'Allowing,' as his combat report records, 'a windscreen-and-a-half deflection,' he opened fire and saw a cannon shell explode on its port wing, leaving a big hole.

That was all he could do. A few seconds later he was left with the impression of a fighter which 'could walk away from a Spitfire with no trouble at all.'

He watched it disappear in cloud, heading for France, and rejoined his section; it was obviously useless to give chase, and Yellow Two needed escorting home.

He had to wait three weeks before he saw a 190 again. Returning from a sweep between Fecamps and Le Treport, the squadron saw seven of them, 2,000 ft below: but twelve to seven were not odds that the Germans were willing to accept. As the Spitfires began to dive, the Focke-Wulfs opened their throttles; and, without having to dive themselves, disappeared rapidly from sight. This was before the Spitfire 5 had its wingtips clipped.

The sweeps continued nearly every day, but without seeing

many enemy aircraft. They were not being drawn: the fighter formations were a taunt to which Goering would not respond; as long as they stayed on the ground, his aeroplanes were safe, and the fighters could not do the damage that the bombers could, so it was not worth going up to try to drive them off; particularly as German aircraft production had fallen, as a result of our bomber raids.

But on the 25th April, while sweeping Hardelot-Hesdin-Le Touquet, about a hundred FW 190s swarmed up to meet the wing in which 602 was flying.

Lacey, leading Yellow Section at 20,000 ft, saw Red Section, which was leading, open fire on one while two more appeared behind them. He called a warning to Red Section and at the same time stall-turned to get in a favourable position; but the two 190s dived away before he could shoot. Red Section had broken and was out of sight; so, with Yellow Two, he went looking for more trade. They saw a pair a thousand feet below and wheeled starboard to move up-sun; then they went in together. In the instant before the Spitfires were in effective range, their quarry saw them and nosed down in a forty-five degree dive, trailing white smoke and pulling away easily. Although the range was 400 yards, Lacey tried a short burst at one from dead astern and the enemy aircraft steepened its dive, while the smoke emerging from it turned dark brown.

Looking up and behind, Lacey saw two FWs above him. He climbed steeply until he was over them, but they both dived away.

He turned towards Le Touquet, and almost at once another pair of FW 190s came in sight, approaching 500 ft below. He reefed into them and delivered a beam attack during which he saw cannon strikes on their rear fuselages; but again they dived and out-distanced him.

When he came in to land he noticed a group of officers standing, as usual, counting the returning Spitfires. But there was something unusual about this group. Even from a couple of hundred feet up, he could see that the Station Commander and his Staff were there, in their best blue; and there was one figure isolated from the others.

When he stood up in his cockpit he observed that the officer standing a little in front of the group of spectators kept turning to address remarks to his companions and that nobody spoke to him first.

The fitter who jumped up on the wing of the Spit. was grinning with pleasure. He said a few quick words which explained everything and as Lacey looked more closely, he recognized the King.

His Majesty had tea in the Officers' Mess, and later Lacey was sent for and presented as the officer who had shot down the Heinkel which had bombed the Palace nineteen months before.

King George VI's first question was: 'How did you know that that was the Heinkel which bombed the Palace?'

'I hadn't the slightest idea that it had been near the Palace, sir. It was the Ops. Room who informed me, when I got back to camp, of the Heinkel's identity.'

Even this royal occasion had a particularly RAF, essentially a Fighter Command, facet. While talking to His Majesty, Lacey noticed that the Mess bar had opened and, with spontaneous politeness, he asked: 'Would you like a drink, sir?'

To which King George replied: 'Yes, please.'

And Lacey, meaning no disrespect, uttered the words which came naturally to every RAF officer. He turned to the barman: 'Two beers, please.'

The King drank his without hesitation, and it was only when Lacey noticed a frown on the face of the C-in-C Fighter Command and some apprehension on the faces of the Staff and the CO, that he gave the matter any thought. He noticed that when the King had his next drink, it was a glass of sherry.

His time with No. 602 Squadron was short. He had earned great fame; and, America having entered the war only five months earlier, British fighting men with outstanding records were being sent on goodwill tours to awaken enthusiasm.

On 25th April, 1942, he was told to prepare for a visit to the USA.

He left the squadron with an assessment of flying ability, signed by Paddy Finucane, of 'Exceptional'.

The rest of April and the early days of May were spent in being briefed on his mission to the States. At the American Embassy he was in the care of the Assistant Air Attaché, 'a wonderful American called Tommy Hitchcock', who was a ten-goal polo player; America's greatest.

Major Hitchcock, American Army Air Corps, had a luxurious flat in Grosvenor Square, where Flight Lieutenant Lacey used to stay. It was a fabulous spell of easy living after more than two-and-a-half years of active service; it was also an introduction to genuine American informality.

One morning, after a celebratory night, the effects of which not even long immersion in a sunken marble bath could quite dispel, Tommy said that he had to go across the square to his office to do a few jobs before they took up where they had left off the previous evening. 'Would you like to come across and meet my boss?'

His guest thought that the least he could do was meet the Air Attaché. He followed Major Hitchcock into a room after a perfunctory knock at the door; and was casually introduced to Mr John Winant, the American Ambassador; who took one look at the two haggard visitors, said 'I don't know what the hell you were doing last night, but I've got the best cure for it,' and produced a large bottle of Bourbon from the bottom drawer of his desk.

Lacey still has the large packet of letters of introduction that Tommy Hitchcock gave him: unopened; because the Treasury cancelled his trip on the plea of a lack of dollars.

It was a sharp disappointment, but getting ready for it had been fun.

He was posted to HQ No. 81 Group as Tactics Officer. And, to mitigate the disappointment, promoted to Acting Squadron Leader on the 27th May 1942. Air Commodore (later Air Vice Marshal, CB) S. F. Vincent, DFC, AFC, the AOC, gave him a generous brief: 'There's a Spitfire established for you as Tactics Officer, and if I see you sitting behind your desk you're not doing your job. Get round the squadrons. Get round the OTUs.' So his new Tactics Officer did just that. His Spitfire 5, unencumbered by cannons, was a fast personal hack and he darted all over 81 Group.

'I wasn't quite certain what my job as Tactics Officer was, but I thoroughly enjoyed it.'

But, after four months, writing training syllabuses palled, despite the abundance of flying and freedom; and when he heard that all the OTUs had to be canvassed for a very experienced Hurricane pilot to volunteer for rocket development at Boscombe Down, he short-circuited the procedure for obtaining the volunteer by attaching himself to Boscombe Down in that role.

Here, he was part of a small unit commanded by a wing commander, with himself, a flying officer and a sergeant as the other pilots. The work was interesting: working up rocket-shooting to a high enough stage of accuracy to get rockets accepted as a weapon by the Royal Air Force.

It was not the safest of jobs and both the wing commander and the flying officer were killed very soon when their rockets went off while still attached to their aeroplanes.

Eventually the unit refined this weapon enough to be able to hit a tank with it, then began experimenting with 40 mm cannons for ground attack. By the time they had got these accepted, it had been decided to start a school, at Milfield, near Alnwick, Northumberland, to train instructors in low attack.

Squadron Leader Lacey was posted there as Chief Instructor. He did not welcome a return to instructing, although it was on rockets and 40 mm cannons: he wanted to go back to a squadron. By now it was November 1942.

Living on a dispersed site, well away from the airfield, in the hard northern winter, with only the modest fleshpots of two small country towns as relaxation from work which was consistently arduous, the members of No. 1 Special Low Attack Instructors' School set about making their quarters almost Babylonian in luxury. Lacey's was an electrical marvel: with an arrangement of lights which would have done credit to the Palladium, heaters, radio sets, a gramophone and a toaster, the room was a web of wires – all emanating from one central light plug. When he switched on this array, all the other lights in the building dimmed while the generators took up the load.

On the 26th March, 1943, he was posted overseas.

Chapter Ten

GET YOUR KNEES BROWN

HE went aboard the SS *Aorangi*, in Liverpool, former flagship of the Canadian-Australasian Lines, not knowing where he was bound.

One of the first things he heard was that a draft of 250 Wrens was coming aboard. The girls appeared while the officers were at dinner. Boarding the ship, they had to walk round the balcony surrounding the First Class Dining Saloon, on the way to their cabins; the handsome parade of legs in black silk stockings was much admired. 'And the finest pair of legs of the lot belonged to a girl called Sheila, whom I got to know quite well during the trip.'

The voyage got off to an exciting start. *Aorangi* sailed to Gourock to join a convoy, which would follow the normal practice of crossing the North Atlantic almost to America, before setting a southerly course; to make things more difficult for the U-boats. But one of her engines needed repair and the convoy sailed without her, so she had to make a lone dash two days later, escorted by three destroyers, by the direct route across the Bay of Biscay. The passage was, perforce, made at high speed; filters had been put in the funnels, to prevent sparks escaping and betraying the vessel's presence in dangerous waters: her very speed was responsible, by reason of the extra pressure of smoke, for blowing these out of position and she careered jauntily down the Irish Sea and into Biscay laying a trail which, at night, could be seen for many miles by German submarines.

This was an experience made doubly uneasy for the RAF aboard: sailing past Brest, with its notorious fighter airfields, was asking for trouble; they were lucky not to find it.

At Casablanca, Squadron Leader Lacey was invited aboard

HMS *Boreas*, one of the escort, by Lieutenant Commander Jones, her captain; a pleasant interlude after confinement aboard a 'dry' ship. Then on to Dakar and at last Freetown where, a week later, the convoy caught up with the *Aorangi*.

The passage from there to Durban was alarming. The sea was strewn with flotsam: hatch covers, furniture, smashed packing cases, overturned lifeboats; all the debris from ships sunk in this sea by enemy action. Most of the passengers had real doubts about reaching their destination.

At Durban Lacey transferred to the SS *Strathmore*, saying goodbye to Sheila who was staying aboard to continue as far as Mombasa.

Bombay gave him his first sight of India. But it was not the fabled Orient which interested him just then: temples, palaces and the strange variety of dress could be investigated later. For the time being, it was the bar at the world famous Taj Mahal Hotel which beckoned. One or two of the younger officers mistook this ornate edifice for the celebrated mausoleum from which it derived its name!

Lacey lost no time in establishing good relations with the Army. The amused, half-incredulous tolerance bordering on contempt which each Service traditionally expresses for the two others, was given extra scope in India, with its peculiar history of 'pukka sahibdom'. Sharing a table in the crowded Harbour Bar with an Indian Army subaltern, Lacey agreeably remarked that he had never before seen chain mail epaulettes worn with khaki-drill; he was, albeit, envious of the youth's immaculate tailor-made uniform, which contrasted vividly with the crushed, travel-stained, store-issue worn by himself and his RAF companions. Indeed, to display his knowledge of Indian military affairs, he added with the joviality permitted to a squadron leader addressing a junior, that this form of dress reminded him 'of one of those fairy tale efforts like Probyn's Horse'.

The youth with the chain mail epaulettes on his khaki drill leaped to his feet, stood at attention, and announced: 'Sir. I *am* Probyn's Horse.'

'Have a drink,' said Lacey. 'And sit down at once.'

Two American flying men at an adjacent table turned

amused faces towards them. One, a burly captain, wore a scowl under his passing grin. 'Goddam Limeys,' he opened, invitingly.

Lacey and his friends pretended not to hear.

The captain belched and repeated: 'Lousy British … godam Limeys … son-of-a-bitching Empire …'

His companion, a tall, thin major with a crew cut, leaned over to Lacey. 'Don't pay any attention, fella. I'm sorry – but the guy's been hitting the bottle. …'

'You surprise me,' murmured Probyn's Horse.

'Yeah, he just got a "Dear John" letter from a British girl in London. They were engaged, see, and now this dame gives Chuck the air for some goddam bird colonel.'

'Rugged,' said Lacey.

'Lousy Limeys,' said Chuck belligerently, 'got yourselves in this war and we have to get you out of it. How come you start something you cain't finish, huh?'

'He thinks you British are decadent,' explained the major gratuitously.

'We are,' Lacey agreed, 'but not so decadent as the Nazis. Or the Italians. Or the Japs. Or … the Americans …'

This penetrated Chuck's neolithic skull about a minute later, and he half-rose, clutching an empty bottle by its neck.

'Sit down,' ordered Probyn's Horse.

'Yeah, siddown, Chuck,' said the major. He turned to Lacey. 'I'm real sorry about this guy …'

'That's all right,' said Lacey, who was getting the germ of an idea, 'move over a bit closer and have a drink; let's see if we can't talk him out of his notion that the British are decadent.'

'Swell,' agreed the major.

Chuck, who had heard the word 'drink', whipped his chair over to the neighbouring table with astounding alacrity, mumbled 'double Scotch' and began to explain how appalling it was that the British would never be able to fight their own wars from now on in.

Two hours and a bottle of whisky later, the captain fell on his face with his arms spread across the table, breathing stertorously.

'Come on chaps,' said Lacey, 'he's out cold.' He stood up and put both hands under one of Chuck's arms.

'Where are we goin'?' asked the Major.

'You'll see.'

They stood on the steps of the Taj Mahal Hotel, while the doorman whistled up a taxi. They crammed into it, waved courteously on their way by Probyn's Horse, who was swaying very gently like a palm tree in a typhoon.

'We want to go to a tatooist,' said Lacey.

The taxi driver, long used to the vagaries of seafarers, was past being astonished by the demands of airmen. He took them. It was in the heart of dockland.

Eight tattooists, working together, surrounded the unconscious American captain for half an hour. When they stood back, revealing their handiwork, the American major whistled in admiring approval.

'Say! You guys sure got your own back there.' Then he began to laugh until he nearly choked.

Lacey and his friends didn't think they'd done so badly either.

Tattooed on the offensive Chuck's anti-British chest was a blazing Union Jack, which for the rest of his life, whenever he took his shirt off, would be seen from a furlong away.

But the major, who had a sense of fair play, and having also been stationed in London deplored his countryman's aggressive Anglophobia, added the finishing touch.

On the way back to their respective units they passed an American Military Police jeep. The major stopped the taxi. He called to the MPs. 'Hey! Soldier! I got an Air Corps captain here you can have – picked him up drunk ...' which was, after all, true.

So far, Lacey had been spared most of the petty irritations of war-time service. But now, after a three-day journey from Bombay to Delhi, to report to Air Headquarters, he found himself returning at once over virtually the same route; back almost where he started from, at Kalyan, near Bombay. His task was to convert No. 20 Squadron from Lysanders to Hurricanes.

Life never seemed to be uneventful when Lacey was around. It was not so much that he precipitated crises, as that events seemed to gravitate towards him. Arrived at the Guard Room at Kalyan, by taxi from the station, he found a crowd of airmen and Indians making a great deal of noise and bustle.

'What's going on here?'

'They're killing a snake, sir.'

Several sweepers with long sticks were prodding and beating a pile of fire wood, while they pranced round it screaming invective. Presently an eight-foot long snake wriggled wickedly into view. The crowd scattered.

'It's all right,' said the newly-arrived squadron leader, 'that's only a grass snake. It's quite harmless.'

It was an impressive arrival. The mob stood staring after him open-mouthed.

His entry into the Mess coincided with a great event. It was the night when the beer ration (1 bottle per man, per week ... per-haps) arrived; four months overdue.

He retired to his bedroom, very late, to see a small snake dart under his wardrobe. Flushed with confidence after having identified the huge grass snake as harmless, borne on a tide of bottled beer, he reached for the small intruder with a convenient walking stick and set about it with his feet. It thrashed and wriggled ineffectually while he trampled it to death. Picking it up by its tail he returned to the bar.

The few who had not yet finished their four months' quota of beer turned in surprise to see him in the doorway with his trophy. An instant later there was nobody to be seen: they had all gone to ground behind the bar counter or the armchairs.

'What kind of snake is this?'

A voice came from the far side of the counter. 'Sir ... that's a ... a krait!'

When he told them that it was dead, they emerged. He still didn't realize that he had caught the most dangerous snake in the subcontinent.

His introduction to service in India was further jaundiced next morning.

On booking into the Mess he had been told that a personal bearer was immediately available: the former servant of an officer who had just gone home. Lacey engaged him, told him what time he wanted to be called in the morning, and thought no more about him. When he went to bed he noticed that the bearer was sleeping on the veranda, and hoped that the fellow was not a snorer.

The next morning, his early tea did not arrive at the time he had ordered. This, he thought, was a poor performance from a bearer who had been so strongly recommended to him. Disgruntled, he shuffled out onto the veranda to investigate. The bearer still lay on his charpai.

'Hey! What's-your-name ... get up, you lazy hound. I want my tea. Cha. Get cracking.'

But the bearer signally failed to get cracking. He just lay.

His master went a bit closer. 'Come on. Or do you want *me* to bring *you* a cupper?'

Still there was no reaction.

He went closer and peered down. Then he jumped back as though he had found another krait, when he saw the hideously swollen empurpled features stiff and lifeless.

That day, helping the Medical Officer, Squadron Leader Lacey inoculated some five hundred natives against cholera. He was used to wielding a hypodermic: his father had been a diabetic and it was often his task to give him insulin injections.

'What with two snakes and a case of cholera in my first twenty-four hours, I never thought I'd get out of India alive.'

It only took three weeks to convert 20 Squadron to fighters, and he was posted to St Thomas's Mount, Madras, to form and command a new unit. It was given a camouflage name of 1572 Gunnery Flight, to conceal the fact that, far from carrying out gunnery training, they were converting six Blenheim bomber squadrons into Hurricanes.

'Some of the Blenheim pilots were so used to having navigators, that they were lost even before their wheels came up.'

Life in Madras was sybaritic. The swimming pool of the Gymkhana Club ... Sunday cricket ... curry tiffins ... sitting in deep armchairs on the riverside at the Addiar Club. But he was unable to convince his relations at home that he was not deep in the jungle, fighting off Japanese, under a Union Jack nailed to a palm tree.

While he was at Madras he received a letter in a hand which had, by now, become familiar. But, instead of an address in Mombasa, it bore one in Colombo. Sheila was now in Ceylon and much nearer to him. From then his trips to Ratmalana, an airfield near Colombo, began and became increasingly frequent. It became a regular weekend visit.

He was sorry when the task in hand was completed. It was marked by a letter from the Air Officer Commanding No. 225 Group, which said: 'I wish to congratulate all those concerned in bringing the conversion training to a successful conclusion. This intricate training operation has called for much hard work, skill and patience, and I am more than satisfied with the way in which the job has been tackled ... I would like you to convey my thanks to Squadron Leader Lacey and his instructors ... who have been largely responsible for the very good results obtained ...'

At just this time, the newspapers at home published 'The New Score Sheet of Fighter Aces'. Some of those who figured on it had not even started their scores at the time when Lacey headed the list.

Kills	Name	
32	G/C A. G. MALAN	Not operational at present
32	S/L FINUCANE	Killed in action
31	W/C BEURLING	Not operational at present
29	W/C STANFORD TUCK	Prisoner of War
28	Anonymous (for fear of reprisals to his family) Polish Sergeant	
28	W/C F. R. CAREY	
27½	W/C C. CALDWELL	
27	F/L MUNGO PARK	Killed in action
27	S/L J. H. LACEY	
25	F/L E. S. LOCK	Missing
25	W/C J. E. JOHNSON	
24	S/L W. DRAKE	
23	F/L M. T. ST JOHN PATTLE	Killed in action
23	F/L G. ALLARD	Killed in action
23	S/L LANCE WADE	Killed in action
22½	W/C D. BADER	Prisoner of War

22 W/C R. F. Boyd
22 S/L Donald Kingaby
22 F/L Kuttelwasher (16 at night)
22 Capt. R. Johnson (USA)
21½ P/O N. D. Harrison
21 W/C J. R. D. Braham (19 at night)
21 W/C Alan Deere
21 Anonymous French Pilot
21 W/C H. M. Stephen
21 S/L A. McKellar   Killed in action
20 G/C John Cunningham (19 at night)
20 Capt. Walker Mahurin (USA)

April saw Lacey's unit transferred to Yelahanka, near Bangalore.

Their task now was to convert all the Hurricane squadrons to Thunderbolts. He was not keen on this job. The Thunderbolt was a big, heavy aircraft; the pilots used to say that the only way in which they could take evasive action was to undo their straps and run round the cockpit.

Ever since arriving in the East he had been trying to get a posting to a squadron, back on operations. He was offered a post at HQ No. 225 Group as Wing Commander Training, but declined this, saying that he did not want to be a wing commander until he had commanded a squadron.

He was feeling despondent at the delay in procuring his return to a battle front. The hedonistic life in Madras had not really pleased him, although he was sensible enough not to spurn it when it was put upon him. Moreover, the training role to which he had been allotted was of utmost importance to future operations.

However, had he been aware of it, his quality was well known in the Command and it was because of his ability that he had been selected for the training of others; his posting to a squadron was ensured as soon as he could be spared.

On the 14th June, 1943, immediately on Lacey's arrival in India, Air Commodore F. J. Vincent, CBE, DFC, AOC, No. 227 Group, had written to Air Commodore A. W. B. McDonald, AFC at Air Headquarters, India:

'I have just seen Squadron Leader Lacey. Quite by accident I saw him wandering round Bombay!! He was one of my Instructors in an OTU at Home. As you probably know, he is one of the outstanding aces of the Battle of Britain. I have forgotten his score, but I think it is round twenty-two or twenty-three aircraft which he has to his credit. He is a very valuable officer in every way. He may not be impressive to look at, but he is a very fearless fighter and he knows most of the tricks in air fighting.

'I was talking to Mellersh yesterday. Although he was not able to disclose plans for the future, I can guess pretty well what is required. In view of these requirements, I suggest that Squadron Leader Lacey would be a most valuable man in the training of those squadrons that are going to be used, so I commend him to you as one of the star turns to be put into any operations which might be planned in the near future. He has had his quota of training in the OTUs at home and he is desperately keen to take an active part in the war again. As much as I would like to have him in 227 Group as an Instructor, I feel that in all fairness to him he should be given first consideration for an active service job. However, that is up to you but I thought I must give you my views, knowing as I do, quite a lot about this officer.'

The reference to Ginger Lacey's comparatively unimpressive exterior was in no way derogatory. He had, since his rest from operations and on the long sea voyage, regained all his youthfulness of aspect. This, added to complete lack of pomposity, condescension or conceit, produced a misleading self-deprecatory impression. In a photograph taken at about this time, on No. 19 Air Fighting Instructors' Course, the twenty-seven-year-old squadron leader with two DFMs looks years younger and infinitely less experienced than the junior officers around him.

Having turned down the wing commander post, he was sent in September 1944 to Third Tactical Air Force HQ at Komila, for re-posting to a squadron.

There was no vacancy on a squadron, so he became Squadron Leader Training, sharing an office with Jimmy Nicholson, Wing Commander Training, who, as Flight Lieutenant J. B.

Nicholson, had won the first Fighter Command Victoria Cross of the war.

Nicholson was a pre-war regular, and had gone to No. 72 Squadron as a pilot officer in 1937. In August 1940, he had recently been made a Flight Commander on No. 249 Squadron. One hot summer afternoon at the height of the Battle of Britain, when his wife was expecting their first child, three Ju 88s appeared about four miles from where the squadron was on patrol.

Nicholson saw and reported them, whereupon his Squadron Commander ordered him to detach and lead his section into an attack. Before the Hurricanes could catch up with the Junkers, twelve Spitfires intercepted them and shot them down. Nicholson, who had not yet fired at the enemy, was disappointed. Turning back to rejoin the squadron, at 18,000 ft, he suddenly heard four tremendous explosions in his cockpit and looked in his mirror to see a Me 110 on his tail. One of the shells from its cannons had ripped through his canopy, sending splinters of perspex into his left eye. His eyelid was almost cut clean through and blood flooded his eye, making it useless. A second shell had burst in his auxiliary petrol tank and started a fire. Another hit his foot and the fourth his right leg.

He broke violently down and found that his attacker had overshot and was now a couple of hundred yards ahead. He gave it a long burst, while both his hands, one on the throttle and the other on the control column and gun button, were blistering in the flames which surged around him. The instrument panel was melting in the heat. With flames roaring around him and searing heat beating at him, he followed the twisting Messerschmitt down, firing at it. It disappeared from sight, diving steeply and also on fire. Then at last Nicholson tried to bale out; but his head hit the framework – all that the flames had left – of his cockpit canopy. He got out, and as he hung in his parachute straps a Me 109 zoomed past; he feigned dead. It had taken him several seconds to fumble the rip-cord open, with his hideously scorched and painful hands. He fell for twenty minutes, and as he approached the earth he recognized that he would drop in the sea; with his wounds, his blood-filled eye and his burns, he would have been unable to survive. He struggled with his shroud lines and guided the 'chute inland: towards high tension cables, he saw, suddenly. Some more manoeuvring, and he was down in a field. He was in hospital for over three months.

Nicholson came from Tadcaster, which is only seven miles from Lacey's home, Wetherby. His greeting to the latter was: 'If you don't write any letters to Tadcaster, I won't write any to Wetherby!'

Office work, even when shared with a congenial fellow-Yorkshireman, was unpalatable and Lacey was impatient to be back in a cockpit; he knew the time could not be far off when he would be given an operational squadron, so he asked to be sent on a refresher fighter course.

On 4th October he began No. 19 Air Fighting Instructors' Course, at Amarda Road. The Air Fighting Training Unit was commanded by Wing Commander F. R. Carey, DFC (later Group Captain), a far-famed and highly successful fighter pilot. This school of his had earned itself as good a reputation as the Central Gunnery School in England itself. 'If anyone knew anything about shooting, it was Frank Carey.'

When the course ended on 6th November, Lacey flew to Imphal for an interview with Air Vice Marshal F. J. Vincent, 'a wonderful AOC', who regretted that he had no permanent squadron command to give him; but sent him to take over No. 155 Squadron while its Commanding Officer was on leave.

Travelling to join the squadron, at the end of the Imphal Valley, by jeep, Lacey was surprised when an almost naked, ferocious-looking Naga stepped from the jungle edge into the dust road and thumbed a lift. The Nagas are notorious head-hunters, whose savage custom continues even to this day; Lacey was not pleased at the prospect of the fellow's company, and almost ordered him out of the vehicle when he caught wind of the appalling stench that clung about him. However, the passenger gave him a gap-toothed grin of appreciation which, even in a head-hunter, did not lack a modicum of charm, and reflecting that the journey would only last an hour, Lacey let him stay.

But the odour grew more sickening with every mile.

Lacey attempted a conversation and found that the Naga had a few words of English.

'Where are you going?'

'To Regiment.'

'What regiment?'

The Naga identified it.

'Why?'

'Give very nice blanket ... red blanket ...'

'I know – hospital blankets ...'

'Yes, sahib. Regiment give very nice blanket.'

'Why? What for?'

'Naga man bring one Japanese man's head – get one blanket ...'

The smell ... realization came ... 'And you've got ... ?'

'I get two blanket, sahib – look ...'

He raised a corner of the tattered old blanket he was carrying. Lacey glanced, then looked away quickly. The two Japanese heads must have been taken days before. In the heat they had not kept well.

No. 155 Squadron, which had Spitfire 8s, was then stationed at Palel. On the day that its temporary CO arrived, the airfield was attacked by Japanese 'Oscar' fighters – Nakajima Ki 43 – and Lacey's log-book has the characteristic entry 'How the hell did the Japs know I was posted here!'

His introduction to his new command was not without a certain dramatic impact and is still well remembered by those who were present.

In the middle of a sweat-sodden morning of blazing heat, when those pilots who were not flying were sprawled around in rickety old chairs in their basha hut crew room, a short, slim, fair-skinned man wearing a bush hat which almost obscured him from view, sauntered diffidently in. He was wearing a khaki shirt, on which the RAF does not sport flying badges or medal ribbons; and as his stores-issue airman's-style shirt had no epaulettes, he was not bothering to display any rank braid.

One or two people looked up hopefully, thinking that his arrival may herald some interesting announcement or at least a pot of tea. The stranger went to the table which stood at one side of the room and began leafing through the magazines and official publications which were strewn on it. Nobody said anything.

The rustle of paper continued. At last, unbearably irritated by prickly heat, boredom and the impertinent intrusion of a presumptuous airman, a burly Canadian flying officer asked: 'Who the hell are you and what d'you want?'

The slight figure at the table half-turned. 'My name's Lacey. I've just come to take over the squadron.'

There was a violent scrabbling of feet and pushed-back chairs as the pilots jumped up respectfully; the word 'sir' echoed about the basha walls.

Some tribute from a group of men so notoriously disrespectful as the veteran pilots on the Burma front. Lacey's reputation had preceded him.

He came to join the battle on this front at a time when air supremacy had already been wrested from the Japanese and the main task of fighter squadrons was to give close support to the advance of the ground troops.

The seige of Imphal had been raised some six months previously and the enemy had been driven from the strategically important ridge on which stands the small town of Kohima. The Japanese Fifteenth Army was retreating. Operations had been delayed by the monsoon, during which 500 inches of rain fell in Assam and 175 inches in Burma. Now, in November, action was again in full spate.

Hurricane fighter-bombers of No. 221 Group had won a fine reputation in the battles, destroying bridges across every watercourse and abyss and harrying the enemy. They played another important role: spraying DDT to kill the mosquitoes and keep malaria down.

The British Fourteenth Army pushed heavily on the Japanese. On the 19th October, Tiddim had fallen; on the 2nd November, Vital Corner; Fort White on the 9th November and Kalemyo on the 14 November. The road to Mandalay and Rangoon lay invitingly ahead.

By this time, the enemy had only some 125 aeroplanes in Burma, of which half were fighters. They gave little opposition to the British and American squadrons of bombers, transport and fighter aircraft which flew unremittingly over Burma and even as far as Bangkok and Malaya.

In the three weeks he spent with 155 Squadron, Lacey flew several fighter patrols and escorted many formations of supply-dropping Dakotas. He felt that he was really back in the war again, but it seemed a tame affair after France, the Battle of Britain and the Blitz. With so few aircraft to be seen by day, the chances of combat in the air were disappointingly remote. Lacey had old-fashioned ideas about the fighter pilot's job, despite his experience of developing and instructing in ground attack. He wanted to see some Zeros and Oscars and try conclusions with them; but this was a different sort of war.

He was to find that it was no less exciting and dangerous.

Chapter Eleven

COMMANDING NO. 17 SQUADRON

ON 23rd November 1944 Squadron Leader Lacey was given command of No. 17 Squadron.

He had fought beside them in France and knew that they had already completed a tour of operations in Burma. They had just returned to the front after a long rest in Ceylon.

The squadron officer and airman pilot strength was as follows:

'A' Flight. Flight Lieutenant D. C. Hindley. Flying Officers H. S. C. Dow (RCAF), C. F. Gerwing (RCAF), D. O. Rathwell (RCAF), R. W. Thompson (RCAF), M. R. Walton (RCAF) and G. A. Pierce. Warrant Officers E. R. Houghton (RNZAF) and J. A. Sharkey (RAAF). Flight Sergeants M. De Silva and J. D. Tollworthy and Sergeant M. Gibson.

'B' Flight. Flying Officers W. J. Detlor (RCAF), W. H. Fell (RCAF), and K. A. Rutherford (RNZAF). Pilot Officers F. D. Irvine and R. B. Connell. Warrant Officers J. Cotterill and A. N. Clark (RAAF). Flight Sergeants A. J. Clarke and N. Ryves. Sergeants F. Holland, D. A. Walde and G. I. Williams.

Flight Lieutenant Cresswell was Adjutant, Flight Lieutenant F. S. Jackson the Medical Officer, Flying Officer R. H. G. Britton the Intelligence Officer and Flying Officer E. R. Hanslip the Engineering Officer.

There was another, very important member of the squadron whom Squadron Leader Lacey now met for the first time. He blinked his eyes disbelievingly and did a 'double-take' as he saw a diminutive figure in khaki shirt and shorts and a bush hat that almost concealed his entire torso, strut past in the company of a group of airmen.

'Who's that?' He pointed.

'That's Chico, sir.'

'And who may Chico be?'

'He's on the strength, sir. Squadron protege, sort of. We found him in Calcutta a couple of years ago, starving and sick: Warrant Officer Williams got him into a military hospital and since then the squadron have looked after him.'

'In what way?'

'Well, the officers all subscribe a small sum every month and he draws it on pay parades along with the rest of the troops. He's been everywhere with us.'

'I see. He doesn't look exactly like an Indian. What is he?'

'He's a Gurkha, sir. That's really why we picked him out in the first place, I suppose. There were a lot of starving kids in Calcutta, but Chico was the furthest from home; and, as I say, he was ill.'

'Good show. Go and fetch him, will you? I'd like to meet the youngest member of my squadron.'

And so the new CO, like everyone else, quickly became accustomed to seeing the cheerful little figure of the eight-year-old Gurkha boy wherever he went: always smiling, always eager to help and as proud of his adopters as though he were himself flying one of their fighters.

Lacey had gone to France with 501 when the greatest bitterness of the campaign there was about to come. He had fought hard against long odds and known that he was part of a defeated force. Now he had come to fight in a theatre where Allied victory seemed imminent and the worst days of the campaign were already behind; but only just.

In order to understand the mood of the men he commanded, the aims of the force of which his squadron formed a part, and his own attitude, it is necessary to know more of the background to future events than has yet been given.

In the early months of the year the Japanese had made a fierce advance, bent on forcing their way across the Burmese frontier into India. Their plan was to drive through the centre of the British front, severing it into western and eastern halves and cutting all lines of communication: and then to annihilate each half, thus freeing the roads to India through Dimapur and Chittagong. In the first phase of this operation Chittagong, an important port in the Arakan, was to be taken; in the second phase the Allied bases of Dimapur and Imphal would fall, and all communications through Assam be cut. Subhas Chandra Bose, the Indian collaborator with the Japanese, was to be established as the leader of a puppet Government as soon as Japanese troops were across the Indian border.

In order to carry out this plan the enemy High Command expected to use tactics which had hitherto proved successful: outflanking the Allied forces so that they must fall back along their lines of supply and communication.

But they had failed to take into account that the Allies now had a very strong air force in South East Asia which would deliver supplies enabling the ground troops to hold their positions and fight back. It was this ability to supply by air that ultimately gave the Allies victory; and every British and American aircraft and flying man and every man on the ground, directly contributed to the one essential weapon and the one means of beating the Japanese in those high, jungle-clad, cloud-wrapped hills and those tortuous, deadly chasms. In country like this the Japanese could live and move as confidently as snakes; the turbulence of cumulo nimbus clouds over the hilltops made flying difficult and dangerous. But as long as the ground troops had the courage and tenacity to hold their positions, the air forces managed to supply them; shewing a comparable bravery and endurance themselves.

In the roasting, humid climate, British and Commonwealth forces battled in the worst conditions to which they could have been subjected. More exhausting than the fierce heat of the desert, because it combined heavy humidity with high temperatures; more deadening than the bitter cold of the Italian winter; further removed than the European Theatre from centres of rest, comfort and contact with normal life: the Far Eastern campaign gave men no respite, few small comforts and, they felt, inadequate recognition at home.

One who never complained about the climate, however, was Chico. To him it was bliss to be taken care of, well fed and housed. The memories of his earlier, bitter years had not been wholly erased and he could still scarcely believe his good luck at the kindness, indeed the spoiling that was lavished on him. It did them all good to see his cheerful, darting little figure full of energy and high spirits when they themselves were worn down by the rigours of the climate.

The Japanese assault started perilously for the Allies. On 6th February, General F. Messervy, who commanded the 7th Indian Division, was in a hand-to-hand fight nine miles behind our own lines in the Arakan. Fighting his way out, he established his headquarters at a small place named Sinzweya. This became known as the 'Admin. Box'.

The resistance of the Admin. Box was the first delay the Japanese met in carrying out their ambitious design.

For weeks before the attack, pilots of patrolling British fighters had reported seeing the lights of our motor transport and the bivouac fires of our troops by night; but had seen no enemy movement. The Japanese had slipped through the jungle and delivered a surprise assault. The support given by their air force amounted to sweeps by 160 aircraft in two days.

In the air supply of the Admin. Box, 2,000 tons of stores were dropped in four weeks. The main ammunition dump was blown up thrice by enemy shells and each time replenished by air. An air strip 200 yards long was cut so that Austers could land to fly out the wounded. Spitfires shot down sixty enemy aircraft. In short, a tremendous all-round flying effort was being made.

On 8th March, the Japanese made two thrusts at Imphal. The importance of this small town lay in the fact that it stood guardian to the main communication route between Burma and India and was our advanced base for the central front. With this place in their possession the enemy would have been able to attack our airfields and supply bases in the Surma valley and break our line of contact with Assam. A huge air lift to Imphal was organized and carried out speedily: in 228 sorties, 3,056 officers and men were brought in, with 50 motor cycles, 40 jeeps, 31 trailers, 8 howitzers, 16 field guns and 100,000 lb of stores.

On 4th April the Japanese attacked Kohima, whose defence saw some of the fiercest fighting in the war. For several days and nights the enemy held one side of a tennis court while the defenders held the other: close quarters indeed. Supplies were dropped daily by Dakotas. In two weeks, four Hurricane squadrons flew 2,200 sorties over the area. Vultee Vengeance dive bombers continually attacked Japanese ammunition and supply dumps.

The supply of Kohima and Imphal and many other places in the densely forested hills went on at high pressure for four months: an average of 275 tons a day was dropped and in June the figure rose to 400 tons. More than 30,000 non-combatant troops, as well as two fully staffed field hospitals, were flown out of Imphal in the month of May.

And over 6,000 airmen were besieged, too. No. 221 Group, at Imphal, formed itself into self-supporting boxes with orders to fight until over-run; there was to be no surrender. Every man carried a weapon and pilots and ground crews slept in fox holes near the aircraft. On top of the vile monsoon weather there were the irritants of dysentery, red ants that bit painfully, black spiders which brought up a burning rash on the skin, and cobras which were ever-present and on which one might tread at any moment in the dark.

Long-range Lightning and Mustang fighters of the US Army Air Corps kept up attacks on forward enemy airfields, while General 'Vinegar Joe' Stilwell's American-Chinese army advanced along the Hukawng valley. A huge air transport mission was completed in early March when, in six days, 9,052 officers and men, 509,082 lb of stores, 1,183 mules and 175 ponies were landed by aircraft and glider 150 miles behind the Japanese lines in north-east Burma: these belonged to Wingate's 'Chindit' Long Range Penetration Group.

By the time the end of 1944 was in sight not only were the Japanese on the retreat, but air offensives had so restricted enemy movement that he scarcely dared stir by day and the daily tonnage carried by rail had been reduced from 750 to 150. Bridges were knocked down and kept broken; roads and jungle clearings were seldom free from observation; everywhere the fighters, bombers and transports were busy.

With so much hardship behind and so much recent success to fortify them, No. 17 Squadron had returned, with a new CO, to play its part in concluding the Far Eastern campaign.

The Squadron was based first at Sapam, in Assam, an airfield near Imphal which had successfully resisted the enemy although the Japanese had occupied the surrounding hills during the siege. They lived in tents and used a runway that had been made by rolling several paddy fields and was several inches deep in dust. Their Spitfire 8s had to take off four at a time, because they whipped up such a dust cloud behind them. They began work at once with defensive patrols and escorting Dakotas on supply drops; but there was morning mist which kept them on the ground until late every day and they were soon ordered to move to Palel.

From Palel, still in Assam, they gave close support to the Fourteenth Army in its advance on Kalewa, which was taken on the 3rd December. Flying low over the valleys and the jungle-matted flanks of the hills, they encountered flak but no enemy aircraft. It was not a very stimulating type of mission; there was little to see and some enemy anti-aircraft fire was actually welcome: it gave them something to shoot back at.

Lacey quickly established himself as an unconventional character.

His Intelligence Officer recalls accompanying him on a jeep drive to Group HQ, which provided him with 'some of the most rapid motoring I have ever experienced. He drove the jeep rather, I imagine, as he flew his Spitfire.' At every roughly repaired bridge, Lacey, jeep and F/O Britton became separately airborne and somehow met again on the far side. The call on Group was followed by supper at the Manipur Club and an even faster drive, by moonlight, back to the airfield.

On 14th December, 17 Squadron left Palel for Taukkyan, in Burma, a strip which the Japs had carved out of the jungle, lying in a lovely setting of hills to the north and west with a wide plain to the south. A little stream ran close to their tents and provided a welcome bathing place.

From here they flew defensive patrols over the bridgehead across the Chindwin, and over the bridge over the Kalewa river, which was the longest Bailey bridge in existence.

Lacey's arrival on the Burma front began a feud with an officer senior to himself for whom he had a deep dislike; and to whom he habitually referred as 'That b ... athlete'. These two had different attitudes to Service life: the one was unconventional and rebellious, the other orthodox and inflexible; frequent clashes would have been inevitable in any walk of life or circumstances.

It was convenient that the dislike was mutual, for The Athlete took care to ensure that as great a distance as possible was maintained between 17 Squadron and his own unit.

A few hours after arriving at Taukkyan, Lacey was approached by his Adjutant, who was smiling broadly. 'Sir, we've had a signal from You-know-who.'

'Oh? What does he want?'

'Wing HQ have just moved to Kalemyo and he says you're to send all available airmen there at once on temporary duty.'

'What for?'

'To help erect a flagstaff and prepare a parade ground.'

'All my airmen are on essential duty. Tell him *I'll* come and help put the flagstaff ...'

The squadron spent many hours on balloon patrol over The Longest Bailey Bridge In The World; a nostalgic duty, reminiscent of home: the sight of the fat silver envelopes swaying in the upper breeze like trunkless but dignified elephants, brought memories of the same silver guardian shapes tethered among the gentler hills and fields of Britain. But reminders of home were no compensation for the boredom of this sort of flying: constantly protecting balloons (that protected the bridge) from aircraft which they knew the enemy had not got.

'If the Japs were going to shoot down those balloons, they would have done so at dawn and been back in Indo-China before we could get after them. But day after day, in the heat, we flew monotonously up and down and when the pilots landed they reported the number of balloons still there: it never varied. Morale was getting pretty low, with our whole effort concentrated on a job like that.'

Lacey had his own way of dealing with the problem. The 3/1 (King George V's Own) Gurkha Regiment was guarding the airfield. No. 17 Squadron's CO issued a Daily Routine Order that all ranks would immediately shave their heads in the Gurkha style; thus becoming 'the first Gurkha squadron in the RAF'.

The novelty and the defiance of Service custom delighted both officers and airmen. It also delighted the Gurkhas. A good relationship already existed between them and the squadron. The regiment had been decimated in the fighting in the Kalewa gorge, and was reforming. In the meantime it defended the air strip. When 17 arrived with a detachment of the RAF Regiment the Gurkhas pointed out to their CO Colonel Bond that, since they had guarded the place when there were no aeroplanes there, it was their right to continue to protect it and the aeroplanes on it.

Told politely that the RAF Regiment had come for that purpose, the little men drew up their own guard roster and continued with their duties as though the latter were not there.

The shaven heads, with the Hindu topknot which the members of 17 Squadron duly left in place on their scalps (to be hauled up to Heaven by!) sent the Gurkhas into paroxysms of laughter.

Lacey's *bête noir* paid him a visit.

'What's this damned nonsense about your men shaving their heads, Lacey?' His eyes opened even more widely as three NCOs walked past. One had a Mohican haircut, another had left a 'V' of hair on the crown of his head, and the third had a 'V' in Morse code – three dots and a dash.

Lacey watched them nonchalantly.

You-know-who barked: 'Abominable.'

'Nothing odd about that,' replied Lacey, casually removing his own bush hat to reveal his bare, topknotted scalp.

A smouldering senior officer put Calcutta out of bounds until hair had been grown again. 'Needless to say we didn't take very much notice of that either.'

But there was plenty to do in the jungle and not many people could get away for a weekend's leave.

The 3/1 Gurkhas, having reformed, were ordered to attack a village called Kin. They gave a farewell party in the Gurkha Officers' Mess. The Subadar Major, a villainous looking warrior with a black eye patch, called at Lacey's office tent to request that the squadron's officers would honour the Viceroy Commissioned Officers' Mess with their presence.

Squadron Leader Lacey consulted Colonel Bond.

'It's quite in order,' said the colonel, 'provided you know what you are doing.'

'What do you mean, Colonel?'

'Well, you know they're rather hard rum drinkers.'

'You know by this time that my little bunch are rather hard drinkers too.'

'Very well, your blood's on your own head. There's nothing in King's Regulations to stop you from drinking with the VCOs.'

So No. 17 Squadron's officers went.

The VCOs' Mess was a cheerful little building, with walls standing two and a half feet high and a roof supported on eight-foot bamboo poles. As they stood, with some formality, inside and made polite conversation over their first round of drinks, the RAF officers could see some thirty Gurkha soldiers squatting on the ground outside. As always, they were laughing and chattering; and taking great interest in what went on inside the Mess.

Lacey rather austerely spoke to the Subadar Major. 'Are your men treating this as a peepshow?'

'No, sahib. They are your orderlies.'

'But what on earth do we want orderlies for?'

The Subadar Major grinned his large grin and said nothing. Lacey found out, the first time he left the Mess to walk across to the latrine. Two Gurkhas rose from the group and accompanied him there and back. Then left him, to rejoin the group, when he returned to the party.

This amiable escort continued for each guest or Gurkha officer who left the Mess. Until, when one of them had decided he would drink no more and sought to leave, he was gently caught by his two orderlies; who held him while he vomited and gently propelled him back into the party. 'He wanted to go home, but they weren't having that: he was still on his feet and so he was put back into the party.'

For the rest of the evening, this fantastic game of 'touch' continued. Each time a rum-laden host or guest sought to weave his queasy route to bed, he was intercepted by two orderlies, helped to be sick, and helped back to the revels. It did not matter how many times any one person was sick: he went on coming back to the Mess. Only ultimate unconsciousness could put an end to this process; whereupon the orderlies took him to bed.

The last three survivors were Lacey, the Subadar Major and one of the Flight Commanders.

This put the seal on the mutual admiration which already existed between the English pilot and the Gurkha officer. Lacey had delighted the latter by taking him up in the Harvard and giving him the full acrobatic treatment: spins, rolls, loops, upward Charlies and everything else that could be done with the aircraft. In appreciation the Subadar Major had presented him with a magnificent kukri. This, thereafter, was a regular part of the squadron leader's jungle escape kit and flew with him on all his operations. It became known in the squadron as the CO's 'Mrs Beeton'; a not unsubtle pun!

On Christmas Day the squadron gave ground support to their Gurkha friends as the attack on Kin went in. The infantry were provided with strips of canvas with which to lay signals for the aircraft which would convey whatever attack instructions they wished to give.

The 3/1 Gurkhas laid only one signal that day: 'Merry Christmas'.

Lacey remarks that there seemed to be something wrong with seeking to kill every Jap you could get your sights on with 'Merry Christmas' to speed you.

Christmas Day was celebrated with a supply drop of tinned chicken and beer.

The communications Harvard came back from one of its trips to Calcutta with toys for Chico and, piled around a tinselled branch from a jungle tree, they reminded the men of 17 Squadron of the family parties at home that they were missing; and gave them at least some vicarious satisfaction as they watched the little boy's face gleam with pleasure and his eyes sparkle as he tore the paper wrappings from each parcel.

On 19th January 1945 the squadron went forward to Tabingaung only ten miles from Jap lines. The move was bedevilled with discomfort. While the advance party slept in the open, waiting for tents to be flown to them, the rear party also slept in the open, with tents ready packed to be loaded on transport aircraft as soon as they came. For six days most of the men slept unprotected from rain, mosquitoes and bugs.

But nobody minded much, because operations began to develop a faster pace. The squadron worked on a three-day rota. One day attacking ground targets under the orders of the Visual Control Posts which were sited right forward and gave the pilots an on-the-spot briefing on what they were looking for. One day flying 'Rhubarbs' against ground targets of opportunity. One day resting. But they usually spent their rest day in flying their own Rhubarbs; and on one of these days, the 28th January, when they flew six Rhubarbs, four damaged trains and one destroyed two trains. At that time there were only thirty trains in Burma.

As if the rain, the snakes and the insects were not irritants enough, there was the intense heat which made the metal of the aircraft so hot that to touch it with the bare skin was to suffer a severe burn.

And the deolali birds. These small, white creatures with red throats would whistle maddeningly by day and night. Starting with a soft, low whistle, they repeated it on a higher note until, after fifteen minutes, they had reached a nerve-tearing shrill-ness that was enough to make tired men, suffering discomfort, scream in sympathy.

One of their operations from Taukkyan had left them all in a mood of disgust and some depression. The Japanese were moving their stores out of Ye U along a long, straight road, on commandeered Burmese bullock carts. The squadron saw this great, slow convoy, reported it and were told to attack.

They made several dummy attacks to give the Burmese drivers time to leave their vehicles and hide in the trees; but these wretched people were ignorant of the devastation threatened by Spitfires which were armed with cannons and machine guns, and they thought that they would be adequately protected if they stopped and hid under the bullock carts.

By this time the Spitfires were getting short of fuel and the attack could no longer be held off. They went in. In less than a minute the convoy was reduced to a shambles of burning petrol, dead and wounded men and beasts, and living torches that ran from under the carts: the four-gallon cans, dripping petrol onto them, had set alight those of the sheltering drivers who were not killed outright. The pilots saw faces turned up towards them in agony and mouths opened to utter screams which, mercifully, were inaudible. Operating against trains, lorries and Japanese troops soon dispelled the horrid memory of this carnage.

In Lacey's log-book is a letter from the Supreme Commander, Lord Louis Mountbatten, dated 26th January, 1945.

'Dear Lacey,

'I shall be most grateful if you would pass on to Rutherford and his co-pilots my thanks for providing fighter escort for my flight from Kalemyo to Ye U on my recent visit to the front.

'I hope that now you are right forward again you will have the opportunities of dealing with the enemy as they should be dealt with.

Yours sincerely,
Louis Mountbatten.'

Lacey's squadron escorted the Supreme Commander many times and never once did he fail to write and thank them.

The Army was hitting hard at Kabwet on the river Irrawaddy, which was wanted as a jumping off place for a river crossing, on the way to Mandalay.

17 Squadron was briefed to attack in front of the advance, for thirty minutes. This would keep down the Japanese fire and enable the British units to advance right up to the enemy positions.

The twelve Spitfires dived time after time, only forty yards ahead of the advancing infantry. To make their ammunition last as long as possible they only fired on one dive in every three. This was a successful manoeuvre, originated by the squadron commander, and kept the heads of the Japanese well down.

Elation over the congratulations which came from the General commanding the operation was still a cause for celebration two nights later when 'after a small party, Lacey and his pilots went to bed. Small parties were not infrequent in 17's Mess. The Harvard two-seat aircraft allotted for communications purposes was flown regularly between whatever airfield the squadron was on, and Calcutta on 'the Hooch Run'; bringing in some thirteen cases of gin a time. It was said never to be on the ground except for refuelling. This produced one distressing crisis, when a King's Messenger arrived and could not be flown on to the next unit. But it produced a lot of gin – and anyone asking for a gin and lime was given his own bottle of each. Even drunk with water that had dripped through a tent, it was not to be scorned: when every other squadron in Burma suffered a gin ration.

On this night, despite the soporific effects of his gin ration, Lacey woke suddenly. He lay for a few moments listening to the familiar jungle noises: the unbroken hum of insects forming a loud background to the shrill calls of birds and monkeys and the occasional howl, grunt or roar of the bigger beasts out hunting. The humid darkness presses in, so that the night seems to have tangible dimensions and to weigh heavily on human bodies, crushing the breath out of them and enveloping them with indefinable threats.

He tried to tune his ears to separate kinds of sound in the

vast darkness and presently one grew dominant: an aircraft engine; and a strange one, at that. He knew it was not a Beaufighter going out on an interdiction mission.

The engine was approaching.

It could only be a Jap.

He rolled swiftly under his mosquito net and dashed out of the tent to stand searching the starlit sky. Screwing up his eyes – which were unwilling to open fully, anyway, from sleepiness and the benefits of the Hooch Run – he quickly spotted the stabbing blue flashes of an exhaust flame from an aircraft which was by now directly over the airfield.

By this time nearly all the tents had emptied and most of the squadron was outside, delivering bitter commentary on the intruder's ancestry and intentions.

They heard it dive over the disused runway along which the aircraft were dispersed. As it hurtled down Lacey saw its silhouette and identified it as an 'Oscar' – presumably one which had been recently stationed on this very strip and flown by a pilot who knew his surroundings intimately even in the dark.

As the enemy aircraft, with its engine bellowing, hurtled down the line of Spitfires, the gallant Squadron Commander made the gesture of emptying his thirty-eight revolver in the general direction of its silhouette. 'It was the only anti-aircraft fire delivered during the whole of the attack!'

Bombs thudded down. Stones and earth pattered heavily on the earth from the eruptions which followed each explosion. They came frighteningly close . . . and closer . . .

A sizzling sheet of flame lit the darkness close at hand and a wave of heat smashed at the group of men. Voices called and flashlights flickered to the sound of running feet. They had to fall back, shielding their faces from the blaze, and watch one of the Spitfires burned out before they could save it.

Officers and NCOs were shouting orders and summoning fire parties. Men ducked as there was a deafening metallic clang followed by a shower of sparks and muffled explosions. Someone shouted: 'It's all right – the-so-and-so dropped a canister of incendiary bombs on the CO's kite, but it bounced off before it opened.'

Had the enemy pilot dropped his bombs from a greater

height he would have destroyed Lacey's aircraft and several more. At is was, he was responsible only for burning out one and damaging two others, because he attacked from so low that his canisters of incendiaries were not fully effective.

Even this frightening night attack had its droll corollary. One of the more cautious airmen had, in preparation for any type of nocturnal danger, dug a trench under his bed. When his friends returned to their tents they found him still in bed: tightly entangled in his mosquito net, into which he had dived when trying to leap into his trench. The more he struggled the more closely was he enmeshed. Of them all, he was in the greatest danger.

But places with unpleasant associations were quickly left behind in the rapid advance and on the 2nd February the squadron was operating from Ywadon. This was a satellite airfield to Monywa, where 909 Wing HQ was.

The latter was notably free of flies. And it must have been the worst possible shaker to the Japanese who had only just been driven out of it, when a formation of Dakotas sprayed the aerodrome with DDT in blatant preparation for and certainty of its imminent occupation by the British. The enemy had taken the hint and moved out immediately.

Laceys first flight from Ywadon was to air test his new aircraft. He had only been airborne a few minutes when a Visual Control Post called him on the R/T. 'Im being shelled.'

'Well ... hard luck!'

'I say again, I am being shelled. Can you please report the gun site.'

'I'll have a go.' Lacey pulled into a steep bank and circled. The thick jungle and the broken landscape of hills and gorges concealed the VCP but presently he made out shell bursts in the area where he had been told to look. 'I can see the shells bursting near you ...'

'Thanks! Did you say near? They're *on*, old boy.'

Lacey climbed a thousand feet and scanned the ground again. Yes. Three or four miles from the VCP's position he saw intermittent clouds of dust spurting up and hanging in the still air. 'OK. I think I've got it.'

He flew straight towards the place and saw at once that the

dust was being thrown up by the muzzle blast of two field guns. Diving into the attack he raked the artillery position with his machine guns and cannon and saw the gunners flung aside like scarecrows scattered by a typhoon as his bullets and shells hammered into them.

The VCP's thanks were quite touching.

The episode must have put Lacey in an exceptionally good humour, because when he got back and was shewn a signal which said that the Japanese might drop parachutists that night to round up the stragglers of their retreating army, he suggested to the IO, 'Spy, you'd better put that Jap flag you've got, on top of your tent so that they'll think it's their HQ.'

'Yes, sir. If you'll swap tents with me.'

But the Japs didn't come that night, and the next day it rained so hard that the airstrip was unserviceable. The rain stopped. Lacey, restless, wandered over to the tent on which he had suggested hoisting an enemy flag as a lure to stragglers and parachutists. Flying Officer Britton looked up. Lacey held a gun in his hand.

'Going to join the infantry, sir?'

'Come on, Spy, I want to try out this Jap rifle. Let's go and see if we can find some game around.'

They headed for the jungle.

Half an hour later, by which time they had killed several large birds for the pot, the IO said: 'Sir ... I have an uncomfortable feeling we're not alone.'

'What d'you mean?' Lacey looked suspiciously about.

The undergrowth parted and six British soldiers darted into view. One dropped to his knees to give the others covering fire, while a companion came intrepidly forward holding a Sten gun at his hip. He halted. 'Where are they?'

Lacey looked puzzled. 'Where are who?'

'The Japs, sir. We heard shooting ...'

'Have one of these vultures – or whatever they are. ... I expect it'll taste OK if you cook it long enough,' said Lacey generously.

Incidents like this, trivial in themselves but a vivid relief from the worries and stress of life on operations in the discomfort of the jungle and the vile climate, became something welcome to talk about; and so the name of No. 17 Squadron and its unusual commander spread far afield.

It reached two flying officers, Don Healey and Don Leighton, in the courtyard of the Grand Hotel, Calcutta, one evening. Just posted to Burma, they were in conversation with some other pilots who had recently come from there.

'Which is the best Spitfire squadron to try to get posted to?'

Their informants were unanimous. 'Seventeen. But you know who commands it, don't you?'

'Yes. Ginger Lacey.'

'Well ...'

'Well, what?'

The experienced pilots exchanged looks. 'Well ... he's fussy about whom he has on his squadron. You don't stand a chance unless you're a bit better than average.'

This made them determined to try. Arrived at Monywa, near Mandalay, they told the tired, overworked officer to whom they reported at the disposal unit they had been told to go direct to 17 Squadron.

'You won't last a week.' But he gave them movement orders and let them go.

At Ywadon, they were directed to the CO's tent.

Entering timidly, they looked around for the legendary Ginger Lacey. There was one naked man asleep on a camp bed. Another, also bare but for a dirty towel around his waist, sat at a folding table, on which stood a bottle of gin, playing patience. His skin was very fair and his hair, which since he had shaved it Gurkha fashion had been allowed to grow again to considerably more than the regulation length, was like damp straw. He didn't look up.

'Er ... excuse me ... excuse us ... we ... we were looking for Squadron Leader Lacey.'

'I'm Lacey.' He was still playing patience, studying his cards, not even glancing at the two smartly attired new pilots.

'We're posted to you, sir.' They tentatively laid their movement orders on a corner of the table. They explained, between them, that Leighton had already done a tour of Italy and shot down $1\frac{1}{2}$ hostiles; and Healey had a respectable total of flying hours on various duties which included instructing.

Lacey continued playing cards. 'All my pilots have to fit in. If you know what I mean. If not, you'll find out. I won't hesitate to post you if I find you aren't up to the squadron's standards – in every way. See that chap charping?'

They stared at the deeply sleeping figure on the other side of the tent. 'Yes, sir.'

'That's Mad Jack the Jungle Quack: the squadron MO. He'll give you a medical when he wakes up and make sure you're up to date with your jabs. OK, that's all.'

Uncertainly, they saluted. Neither of them had ever experienced an interview remotely like this one. They were at the tent's exit when Lacey spoke again, still in the same quiet, unemphatic voice. 'By the way, there is no such thing as an accident on this squadron. So if you have one, you'd better kill yourself at the same time.'

There was another silence. Correctly assuming that this time they had been dismissed, they went wonderingly to their quarters. At the first opportunity they asked one of the Flight Commanders about the Squadron Commander's attitude to accidents. He replied dourly. 'I'll give you an example. One of the pilots hit one of the oil drums that mark the strip, when he was coming in to land. He's experienced, all right; but the CO immediately sent him back to India for further training. We don't expect him back for at least two months.'

They had one more immediate shock to come, next time they met Lacey. 'Incidentally, I gather you're about due for promotion to flight lieutenant, both of you. When it comes through, you'll continue to wear the rank badges of flying officers. The only flight lieutenants on my squadron are my two Flight Commanders. Understand?'

They were beginning to understand.

Everyone on the squadron had to earn his place and the right to be considered fit to hold it. Lacey could look after himself and he expected everyone else to be capable of doing the same: especially when they flew as No. 2 to him. But, in many ways, it made life simpler.

Healey, flying with him on a low level sweep, reported tracer coming from a palm tree standing by itself; and got permission to break off to investigate, with instructions to rejoin.

Pulling away, he opened fire on the tree-top and saw a man's figure, blasted out of it, tumble fifty feet to the hard ground.

Lacey was nowhere in sight and eventually Healey landed alone, before his leader. As soon as the latter was down, he was met by an apologetic No. 2, who had already convinced himself that he would be sent away from the squadron for losing his leader. Lacey silenced him. 'That's all right, Healey. Any patrol which arrives back within fifteen minutes of each other must have been a good one!'

But 17's jokes were not always kindly. To one of the pilots is attributed an acid comment on the R/T which can have done nothing to encourage the friendship of the Indian squadrons. Flying on an operation during which they had all been briefed to maintain R/T silence, a faltering Indian voice was heard.

'Hallo Wiper Leader. I say, what colour are we: Blue Section or Green?'

There was no answer. Wiper's Indian leader was not going to break silence.

The same voice bleated again. 'I say, Wiper Leader, are we Blue or Green?'

An unidentified 17 voice, in exasperation, gave him the answer. 'You're black, you so-and-so.'

There was an injured quality about the ensuing silence.

Chapter Twelve

FROM BURMA TO MALAYA

THE operations of No. 17 Squadron were maintained at forcing pace.

The pilots flew well over 2,000 operational hours in February 1945. During one twenty-four hour period, they shot down three Japanese aircraft: the only ones they were to see during four months.

The 'regimental' Athlete with whom Lacey maintained a running battle, visited the squadron during the height of this period of activity: and complained that a passing corporal had come on duty unshaven. 17's CO was pleased to point out that the man in question had been working without a break for the past twenty-eight hours. If the men worked long, wearying hours, it was not without recognition from their Commanding Officer. When there was less work to be done he would put a three-ton lorry at the disposal of those who were free and let them go where they pleased for recreation. The Athlete thought it would have been better if he held parades.

Most of their work was patrolling over the bridgeheads established over the Irrawaddy by the Fourteenth Army, and carrying out offensive sweeps over Japanese troops and positions.

The Spitfires had to be inspected after every thirty hours of flying, and the ground crews would work all day and night without rest if necessary.

Ground strafing had an exhilaration of its own and offered some variety. It may not have been the role for which fighter pilots felt themselves traditionally cast and it certainly lacked the thrill of combat aerobatics; but it had its points. Sometimes they flew as low as twenty feet above the ground with palm trees reaching up ten times as high flashing past their wingtips. Often they had to dive steeply into a small clearing and pull up vertically to climb out of it without ploughing into the jungle. Now it was a gunsite, next a convoy of trucks, last time perhaps some railway wagons, that they fired at. When they gave close support to the infantry they could see them charge forward in the wake of the Spitfires' shells and bullets; and they could see the Japs streaming out of their foxholes and the undergrowth to go rolling over and over as their fire swept witheringly over them.

Lacey still has, as a memento, some palm leaves which he scooped up with his radiator when attacking a small group of basha huts used by the Japanese. After attacking three times without setting them on fire, he held his run a trifle too long the fourth time and skimmed through the top of a tree on his way out.

On the 18th–19th February the Squadron enjoyed several memorable events.

The first occurred when Pilot Officer Connell, on an air test, heard an Operations Controller on the R/T vectoring another Spitfire towards a Japanese reconnaissance aircraft whose exact position was unknown.

Willing to lend a hand, Connell, who had just passed through a few exciting moments himself, called: 'What is reported position of Hostile?'

'About Angels thirty, over Monewa.'

Connell, who had apparently picked up one or two of Lacey's habits, informed the Controller nonchalantly: 'That is where I happen to be at the moment.'

'Whacko!' said the Controller excitedly, 'Can you see a Hostile?'

'Yes. I can see it. It's an "Irving".'

'Are you going to attack?'

'What – again?'

'Message not understood . . .'

'The "Irving" is on fire. I've just shot it down. . . .'

Their least favourite senior officer came to call; but even his sourness could not spoil the effect of this casual victory.

The pilots had adopted the widespread RAF habit of wearing bright scarves to soak up the sweat that plagued them; and, of course, there was rivalry to wear the gaudiest.

The exalted visitor did not approve. 'Really, Lacey, can't you stop your squadron from going around dressed like Harlequins?'

Lacey said that he wouldn't dream of trying. And ostentatiously pulled his own dazzling neck cloth from a pocket and knotted it about his neck.

The next morning Lacey was on dawn patrol with Warrant Officer Sharkey as his No. 2. He liked flying dawn patrols because his fair skin was painfully susceptible to the heat and later in the day the Spitfires' cockpits were like ovens. Sharkey, an Australian, was his regular No. 2 and he describes him as the finest No. 2 he has ever flown with. 'Whatever I did, I knew I'd never lose Sharkey. He just stayed on my wing-tip like glue.'

The sun was coming up quickly and not far ahead Lacey spotted a dozen flitting shapes in the sky.

'Red Two. See them? Twelve o'clock, about 2,000 ft below.'

'Yeah, I've got 'em.'

'Let's go.'

They jettisoned their long range tanks and opened their throttles. The Spitfires had great superiority of speed over their prey, which Lacey and Sharkey recognized as 'Oscars' the Japanese Army fighter.

The tactics of the 'Oscar' when attacked were well known. It was a small aircraft with an amazing rate of turn. On being attacked, the 'Oscar' pilot would not increase his speed, but on the contrary, reduce it. Watching in his mirror, he would wait until he saw the flashes at his attackers' gun ports which indicated that it had opened fire. Even turning at this last moment, the 'Oscar' could whip round fast enough to deliver a head-on attack which took its pursuer by surprise and at a lethal disadvantage.

As the two Spitfires dived on the twelve Japanese fighters the pilots saw the latter's combat flaps go down: they had been spotted. The Spits were by now gaining at about 150 mph and the 'Oscars' evidently gauged that they had better not wait for gun flashes before turning. Just before Lacey and Sharkey were in range, the formation in front began to turn: except for the last aircraft, which lingered. Then, a few seconds too late, it followed the others; but not in a tight enough turn.

Lacey touched off a half-second burst with his cannons.

He saw two explosive bullets slam into the 'Oscar's' starboard wing; one hit the fuselage; and one hit the perspex hood, which was shattered into a myriad glittering fragments. The little fighter rolled onto its back and went into a vertical dive. The two British pilots shot up in a fast climb to get above the rest of the enemy, who were approaching rapidly from abeam. Looking down they saw Lacey's victim hit the ground with a streak of flame and a gout of smoke.

The enemy now split into two sections, obviously hoping that the Spitfires would attack one of them; thus leaving themselves vulnerable to the guns of the other. But Lacey led Sharkey home.

When he had made his combat report, the leader turned to his No. 2. 'Did you get anything? Did you shoot?'

The Australian shook his head. 'No. Why should I shoot? I was just watching you – lost in admiration!'

Looking back, his CO says, 'Not a very useful No. 2 that time! But I'd still rather fly with Sharkey on my wingtip than any No. 2 I ever met during the war.'

They were in the basha crew room with the rest of the pilots, reliving the episode, when a worried-looking flight sergeant fitter came in.

'Excuse me, Squadron Leader Lacey, sir ...'

'What's your trouble, Chiefy?'

'Are you sure you got that Jap, sir?'

'Ask Mr Sharkey! Anyway, why ask at all?'

'Well, sir ... it's just that you can't have hit him, sir ... you've only used nine rounds of cannon.'

Lacey lit a cigarette, taking his time. In silence, his pilots watched him. He did not even look at the flight sergeant. 'Oh, really, Flight? As many as nine? You surprise me!'

In the roar of laughter that met this retort, the red-faced NCO fitter withdrew and a new Lacey story was born to go on its rounds with all the others.

One of these was that he and Flight Lieutenant Jackson, the MO, used to extract the gold teeth from all the Japanese corpses they found and that Lacey would take them to Calcutta from time to time where an agent sold them! There were even people who could describe to you the little canvas bags in which these two officers stored the Japs' gold fillings.

Another had Lacey selling the broken glass from his jeep's tail light to an American colonel who had never been further east than Calcutta, as 'genuine uncut Burmese rubies'.

The doctor was something of a character in his own right. An apocryphal story about him alleged that he used to collect Japanese skeletons, clean them, and dispatch them to the respectable vaults of Cox & Kings, in Calcutta: to take home for sale to medical schools!

Lacey did nothing to discourage the yarns that were told

about him: a legendary Commanding Officer was something which made the squadron feel different from and superior to others, and anything that helped to keep morale high was acceptable to him.

On the same day that he destroyed his first and last Jap (the only one he ever saw when in the air himself) Pilot Officer Irvine brought down another 'Oscar': three in twenty-four hours; there was nothing that could have pleased Lacey more.

A few days later, Flying Officer Rutherford claimed a probable 'Oscar'.

At the end of February the enemy was driven from Meiktila and the patrolling pilots saw the town in flames with smoke rising to a height of 5,000 ft.

On the 2nd March, 17 Squadron began to carry out patrols from the Meiktila airfield. But although the Fourteenth Army now held the town, they had to regain possession of the air strip every day: they lacked the troops to occupy it during the night. At each sunset, the force withdrew to the protection of its barbed-wire box; the Japanese, knowing the airfield was left undefended, stubbornly returned to it. With first light, an attack was put in (usually by the RAF Regiment) to clear them out. As soon as the airfield was reported to be back in British hands, No. 17 Squadron flew in. Invariably, they had to help in removing enemy corpses from the runway.

The RAF Regiment won bloody renown in the fierce fighting for repossession of the landing ground every humid morning. One day that the squadron remembers, one of the aircraft dispersal bays was full of bodies of RAF Regiment officers and airmen awaiting burial.

The Japs were dealt with with a bulldozer. First a pit was dug, then the corpses were scooped into it and the earth was bulldozed back.

The sourly cloying stench of fast-decomposing flesh hung over the strip and a great area around it.

One morning, the signal that Meiktila airfield was fit for operation came prematurely. Lacey was the first to land. As he turned at right angles to the runway towards his dispersal bay he heard a loud report unpleasantly close at hand and jerked his head round to look for the gun, at the instant that there was a metallic thud and his aircraft shook. Sparks flew from the propeller spinner. A second later, a 75 mm shell that had passed through the spinner exploded fifty yards away in an ugly grey, orange-streaked boil of steel, smoke and flames. A couple of hundred yards from the end of the runway, dust was settling around the gun which had fired it. The strip was clear, but an enemy still commanded it. 'I never taxied so fast in my life: I went into an aircraft bay with my tail wheel off the ground.'

If the gun had fired three seconds sooner it would have sent its shell into his engine; a second later, and it would have hit the cockpit beam-on.

On the 9th April the squadron moved permanently to Meiktila, which was no longer menaced by the enemy at night. There were two pleasant lakes nearby, which provided welcome swimming; for a while. It had to stop after a few days, on account of the Japanese bodies which were floating to the surface: wearing full kit, they had to grow very bloated indeed, with the gas of decomposition, before they were buoyant enough to reach the surface.

Four days after the move, Lacey was stung three times by a scorpion, which produced a huge, poisoned swelling on his leg, kept him off flying for a week; and did not put him in the best of tempers: as Flying Officer Healey and Flight Sergeant De Silva found out.

These two pilots, on patrol at 5,000 ft behind Japanese lines, some fifty miles north of Rangoon, were maintaining positions about a mile apart; they were both weaving, constantly searching the sky and keeping a watch on each other. Healey looked down and saw a squadron of Mosquito bombers hedge-hopping towards Rangoon. Approaching them head-on at the same low level was a Spitfire. With the morbid curiosity of every pilot who sees a situation fraught with problems developing, he looked on with interest for what he thought must be an inevitable tangle. But the Spitfire skimmed over the top of the Mosquitoes without providing any spectacular entertainment.

A minute or two later, looking towards his No. 2, he saw De Silva pull up in a steep turn and bear down towards him in an obvious attack. Wondering why De Silva had elected to make a dummy run at this moment, he turned to look behind and saw the same Spitfire which had barely escaped collision with the Mosquitoes, climbing up to get on his tail. De Silva had seen it, mistaken it for a Hostile, and was about to shoot it down.

In quick alarm, Healey called his partner on the R/T. 'Don't shoot! It's a Spit.' And De Silva broke directly overhead.

The strange Spitfire drew alongside and the two 17 Squadron pilots read the identifying letters on its fuselage. It belonged to Lacey's loathed Athlete! He waggled his wings and peeled off, leaving them to continue with their patrol.

Lacey summoned the leader to his office tent when they landed. Healey stood formally in front of him, at attention.

'I've just had a caustic message from You-know-who. He reported that you were not keeping a good look out and he could have shot you down. I'm damned annoyed that, of all people, this should happen to one of *my* pilots.'

'It didn't happen, sir.'

'He says it did.'

'Rex De Silva spotted him on my tail, just before I did, and was already making an attack on him, thinking he was a Jap, when I told him not to shoot.'

'Are you sure?'

'If you'll send for De Silva, sir, he'll tell you his story.'

Flight Sergeant De Silva came, and corroborated his leader's account.

Lacey dismissed them so that he could have a private telephone conversation with the athletic and mistaken senior officer. As Healey ducked out of the tent he heard his name spoken in the CO's habitual monotone. 'Don.'

'Yes, sir?'

'Pity you didn't let Rex shoot the so-and-so down.'

Meiktila provided a good source of supply for the enterprising airmen and NCOs on the squadron who used to take Japanese souvenirs to Calcutta when they went on leave and sell them to envious base area officers and troops, British and American, who had never been in the combat field. Enemy uniforms with medals were much prized, firearms and swords fetched a good price; and 'captured flags' fashioned from the fragments of supply parachutes were impressive – except that the Japanese characters printed on them probably meant 'fragile', 'this side up' or 'to be used before next New Year'.

Activity at Meiktila was mounting. When the squadron had first come here they had set up their tents in a thunder storm which had swamped many of them as soon as they were erected. The day after they had suffered a severe dust storm. And by now, three weeks later, the aerodrome was the main supply terminal for the advance on Rangoon: in incessant noise and dust, transport Dakotas were taking off and landing every few minutes. There was little comfort and the din made sleep difficult, but everyone was happy in the feeling that they were in the forefront of a victorious advance.

From Meiktila to Thedaw, for a few days; remembered for the stream running behind the domestic tent lines, where the bathing was safe and clean. Then on to a temporary strip code named 'Tennant' in honour of the East's most famous brand of beer.

It was, in a way, good to get away from Thedaw which had a poor runway only 600 yards long and 25 yards wide, full of holes and soft patches. But the arrival at Tennant was accompanied by a warning that a thousand Japanese were at large in the area: probably on their way to attack the strip.

The squadron dug trenches and slept near the aircraft that night, with rifles and revolvers at hand. But the only Jap who approached them dropped his rifle and fled when challenged by the guards.

It was a night not entirely free of excitement, however.

While the ground crews slept near the aeroplanes, the pilots, who had to conserve their energies for the next day's flying, were in their tents.

It was just before the Monsoon, when the nights are pitch black.

Lacey woke with a start to the loud drumming of heavy rain on the canvas. He lay gasping for breath in the stifling heat, then stirred himself to crawl out of bed as the rain came splashing over his naked body. Groping his way towards the tent flaps, he pulled them down and laced them to keep the rain out.

Then he thought of his companion, the MO, who slept at the other end of the tent. It was too dark to see, but 'being at heart a very decent chap, I thought that while I was out of bed I might as well go and lace up the Doc's flaps also.'

Easing his way silently along the tent, holding his hands before him so as to avoid walking into the centre pole, he touched warm, sweaty bare flesh.

He recoiled as fast as if he had put his fingers in a tiger's jaws. The Japanese, at night, used to infiltrate into Allied lines wearing only a loincloth. And there were a thousand of them abroad this very night.

With his heart thumping, he flung himself at the intruder, hurled him as violently as he could across the tent and scrambled back to his bed to grab the revolver which was under his pillow.

Somewhere in the darkness he heard softly spoken but out-rageously angry words in English; as the MO, who had also risen to secure the tent flaps, groped under his own pillow for his revolver.

'That you, Doc?'

'Who the hell d'you think it is?'

'I thought you were a Jap.'

'Was it you? *I* thought *you* were a Jap ...'

'Yes ...'

'I was trying to find my thirty-eight to take a shot at you.'

'Same here!'

They were patrolling over Rangoon every day, and at last came the morning when the city was in flames as the Four-teenth Army shelled and the Allied Air Forces bombed it. 1st May, 1945. Not long after, the patrolling pilots saw, in huge white letters on the roof of the gaol, the message 'Japs gone'. And, to anthenticate the information and dispel suspi-cion that it was enemy bait to draw the forces into Rangoon, another message was painted on an adjoining roof: 'Extract digit'.

Soon after the fall of Rangoon, 17 Squadron were told that

they would be withdrawn from Burma, to re-equip with Spitfire 14s in preparation for the invasion of Malaya.

On the 2nd June, Squadron Leader Lacey flew to Madura, in southern India, to ensure that the station was ready to receive his squadron. It took him five days, via Calcutta and Madras.

Sheila, meanwhile, had been transferred from Colombo to the Fleet Air Arm station at Coimbatore, only 120 miles away. Two days after arriving at Madura he flew over to see her. This visit would have surprised his squadron if they had known about it: but they did not even suspect that their commander had an amorous interest; even the MO, who had shared a tent with him since he came to the squadron, was not admitted to this confidence.

Presently the rest of the squadron arrived at Madura. But where were the new Spitfires? By the end of the month, they had not appeared. A romantic impulse stirred in Ginger Lacey. The idea of a traditional wedding attended by a horde of relations and friends, embarrassed him; he was delighted to find that the prospect had a similar lack of appeal for Sheila.

'So at the end of June I slipped over to Coimbatore, picked up Sheila and we went up into the hills to Kodaikanal; on the 8th July, much to everyone's surprise, we walked into the club there and announced that we had just got married. Nobody would believe it, of course, but when eventually we convinced them, they gave us a wonderful time. They even insisted on giving us a bungalow to spend our honeymoon in.'

The squadron, to whom he had broken the news, assembled in the Madura Club on the night of his expected return, to welcome the bride. Characteristically her husband decided to postpone the occasion.

But on the next day, the 16th July, he returned to his command.

The Spitfire 14s had arrived. Lacey took his off to try it out. He had a theory now that the most dangerous periods in a man's life are when he has just assumed a new responsibility such as a wife or a child: super caution overrules his instincts and acquired skills.

The new Spitfire was, to his touch, like a Stradivarius to a violinist. Out of sight of the airfield, he found such joy in handling the machine that he came back in a long, swallow dive across the airfield with the intention of doing a loop over base before landing.

'Half way up the loop, I realized that I had gone into it much too slowly and I wasn't going to make it. As she approached the top of the loop, on her back, I was frantically trying to roll her out because I knew she was going to stall. And of course with full aileron on, not only did she stall inverted but she spun inverted. I was only at 2,500 ft. I knew what to do, but it took some doing. I forced her nose down, still upside-down, and let her pick up speed. When she had enough speed, I rolled her out. By that time, I didn't have very much height left. I've never been closer to being killed.' So much for the extra caution of the newly married fighter pilot.

Preparation for 'Operation Zipper', the invasion of Malaya, demanded a high standard of airmanship: No. 17 Squadron would have to fly off a 'Woolworth' carrier – a merchant ship equipped with a flight deck that allowed no room for mistakes.

On 15th August, the Japanese laid down their arms.

The atomic bomb had been dropped on Hiroshima on the 6th August, and it was obvious that the armistice must come very soon. In the meanwhile, the Station Commander had gone to Bombay on temporary duty, the Wing Commander Flying also had to leave the station for a few days, and command passed to Squadron Leader Lacey who was the senior Squadron Commander.

Foreseeing the celebrations which would follow the Japanese surrender, he laid down stringent rules to avoid all types of accident. No transport was to be driven except by Indian drivers with armed escorts; all pyrotechnics and arms were locked in the armoury and he kept the key himself; all aircraft were grounded.

The end of the war was announced and a monumental party began. Well on in the night one of the pilots (not from 17 Squadron), well nourished by gin and beer, produced a two-star Very cartridge he had concealed and fired it into the sky.

Ten seconds later, the pyrotechnic landed on a basha hut.

Within five minutes, forty-two officers' quarters and three lorries had been burned to the ground.

In consequence, five officer pilots had Summaries of Evidence taken against them and were awaiting probable Courts Martial when their squadron was posted to Hong Kong, leaving them behind. And it happened that Lacey's squadron was exactly five pilots short when the time came to embark for Malaya. 'As you know, it's always the good pilots who are involved in slight breaches of discipline.'

Lacey ordered all five of them to be on the runway with their bags packed when the transport Liberators came to embark the squadron's equipment for China Bay and the carrier. The last Liberator was only half full and he ordered them to board it.

By the time he got them to Singapore, nobody could remember much about them; he informed HQ Air Command South East Asia that he had these pilots with him and asked for them to be formally posted to his squadron: they were.

'I got rather a rap over the knuckles for kidnapping these pilots, but at the same time I got a pat on the back for making sure that my squadron arrived in Malaya fully up to strength: which I could not have done in any other way.'

'Operation Zipper' became 'Exercise Zipper'; it could not be stopped entirely, because a huge invasion force was gathering all over the world and it was simpler to let the arrangements stand than to try to halt the preparations. On 30th August, the squadron flew to China Bay, in Ceylon, to be embarked on HMS *Trumpeter*.

Taking off from Madura, he had a tyre burst. The Spitfire wheels had split hubs which were kept in place by the air pressure in the tyres. When a tyre burst, the wheel came off. An hour and fifteen minutes later, Lacey was faced with the problem of landing at China Bay: either with his wheels up, on the aircraft's belly, doing considerable damage; or on one main wheel and the tail wheel. If the latter method did not succeed, the aircraft would almost certainly overturn.

Commander Flying, on the R/T advised him strongly to land wheels-up.

Lacey decided that he could put his aeroplane down sucessfully with its wheels down.

In the event, he did. So gently that not even the propeller was damaged. A dozen men ran out to him on the runway. Six sat on one wing and six heaved underneath the other. A spare Seafire wheel was fitted, and he taxied to his dispersal point.

If landing at China Bay had been difficult, taking off from the *Trumpeter* in the Malacca Straits promised to be almost impossible. The ship was only 420 ft long; Lacey, leading the way, had six Spitfires lined up behind him and only 350 ft of deck in front of him. Every knot of head-wind was equivalent to 10 ft of runway, but it was a dead calm day and the only wind over the deck was what could be achieved by the ship's speed. Commander Engineering produced a phenomenal $17\frac{1}{2}$ knots ('I don't know what he was doing – burning the Wardroom piano, I think') which gave them half a knot more than she had done even on her acceptance trials. The navy did them proud, and despite some frightening moments when some of the pilots sank below the level of the flight decks as they left it, all twenty Spitfires were got off safely.

They landed at Morib. The Army should have been there first, to occupy the airfield, but were bogged down on the way. The Japanese major in command surrendered his sword and the airfield to Squadron Leader Lacey.

Three days later the squadron did a fly-past at the Japanese surrender at Kuala Lumpur. By that time the Army had arrived at Morib; and with them came the rations: until then, the squadron had been living on the CO's signature in all the Chinese eating houses round about. They were sorry to see the rations come up.

On 23rd September, 17 went to Singapore Island; first to Tengah then to Seletar.

There was very little flying to do, but plenty of swimming, fishing and football. Already the months in Burma belonged to another era.

From Singapore to Kuala Lumpur. And now the good news that they were destined for Japan. It was a fitting destination for a squadron which fought its way back into, and through

Burma after having taken part in the withdrawal from there in 1942.

They had to say good-bye to Chico at last. A heart-rending parting for the child and for the men who had gently cared for him for four years. But they left him in the charge of the RAF station at Butterworth, northern Malaya, with a generous gift of money in safe-keeping for his maintenance and his future.

This time, they embarked in HMS *Vengeance*. But her captain was not prepared to steam at full speed in the Inland Sea of Japan, which had been heavily mined by both the Japanese and the Allies, so instead of flying their Spitfires off they watched them taken off by lighters. No. 11 Squadron, their old friends and rivals, were aboard with them. Immediately each had an aircraft ashore there was tremendous competition to get it ready to be the first Spitfire to fly over Japan.

Chapter Thirteen

THE FIRST SPITFIRE OVER JAPAN

THE race to get the Spitfires serviceable was close run.

As Lacey taxied out, he saw another Spitfire approaching the other end of the runway from No. 11 Squadron's dispersals. He knew that the pilot must be Squadron Leader Mac-Gregor, 11's CO.

'I was lucky. I was facing into wind.'

Both pilots opened their throttles simultaneously and bore down on each other head-on. Neither gave way. Lacey, taking off up-wind, got airborne first and scraped barely three feet over his rival Squadron Commander's head.

No. 17 Squadron had put the first Spitfire over Japan. 30th April 1946.

Their base at Iwa Kuni was not far from Hiroshima and Lacey went to have a look at the effects of the atomic bomb. He was appalled by the devastation: the only reinforced concrete building in the city still stood, although it was gutted. The rest of the town was flat. Whole lengths of railway line with their sleepers still attached had been tossed half a furlong from their embankments.

On the 6th May 1946 he said good-bye to his squadron and embarked for Singapore on his way to England where Sheila had preceded him.

He was sorry to leave the squadron, but not reluctant to leave the Far East. The days when a legendary, independent fighter commander had led a famous squadron to victory had already gone, never to return. The man who had been known all over India, Assam, the Arakan and Burma for his strong individuality and his effectiveness in getting things done in an unorthodox way and with the minimum of fuss, had played his part. The war was over, Japan was occupied; and men like Ginger Lacey belong where Mannock, Macrudden, Ball and Billy Bishop belong; where Bader, Cobber Kain and Screwball Beurling belong. When the nation is in danger we make much of them. When the staid days of peace rule our lives we are not always as grateful as we should be.

They are men who hate war as much as the rest of us, but who are especially equipped for it by nature; and, it may be, too well endowed with enterprise and bravery for the conditions of peacetime, which restrict their personalities.

Let two pilots of No. 17 Squadron sum it up.

'The CO's courage and exploits are well known.'

And, 'He didn't show off with fancy flying, but his reputation (well earned) was for bags of guts and being a wonderful shot. Surely the two most wanted attributes in a fighter pilot.'

Chapter Fourteen

NEC DEUS INTERSIT, NISI DIGNUS VINDICE NODUS

AIR MINISTRY had no flying jobs to offer which would allow an acting squadron leader to retain his rank. But there was a post going in the Air Ministry itself, and Acting Squadron Leader Lacey joined the Directorate of Accident Prevention. Six months later, when this was made a Deputy Directorate, with the consequent reduction in establishment, he was the first to ask for a posting ('I'd have gone as a sergeant pilot, let alone as a flight lieutenant'). Being immured in a London office was not what had attracted him to the air force.

Even as late as March 1947 a few priveleges still came the way of ex-squadron commanders with twenty-seven confirmed victories over enemy aircraft to their credit. He was allowed to choose his posting and elected to join No. 72 Squadron at Odiham, Hampshire, which was commanded by Squadron Leader 'Buck' Courtney, who had been a Wing Commander Flying in Burma.

On 72, which was equipped with Vampires, he flew jets for the first time; and found it much simpler than flying a Hurricane or Spitfire.

He soon forgot the boredom of office life in the return to the camaraderie of a squadron and the pleasure of formation flying, aerobatics and practise interceptions: the latter under the close control of Ground Controlled Interception stations, which he would have welcomed in 1940–41.

On 29th May he was granted an Extended Service Commission; but in the Aircraft Control Branch, as a Fighter Controller. He immediately applied to remain in the General Duties (Flying) Branch and was allowed to stay with the squadron. He was still there in March 1948, when he was posted to begin his duties as a Fighter Controller.

There followed periods at the School of Fighter Control and on a GCI station, which ended on 8th December 1948 when he was granted a Permanent Commission in the GD Branch.

In February 1949 he went on a conversion course to Meteors and thence to No. 43 Squadron at Tangmere, as a Flight Commander.

August 1949 saw him on his way to Hong Kong as an acting squadron leader to do a tour in Fighter Control. And there he added, through no conscious effort, to the many stories already told around his name.

One of these will serve as an exemplar.

Squadron Leader Lacey, commanding a GCI station in the New Territories, was due to visit Kai Tak, the main airfield and Administrative HQ, early one morning. The Adjutant spoke to him in the Mess the previous evening.

'Sir, I've just taken on a new cook for the Mess ...'

'Thank goodness. It's about time. I don't eat as much as you other chaps, but it seems to me the meals have been like par-boiled hemp, lately.'

'Yes, sir. Well, this new cook has to be medically examined and security cleared. Would you mind taking him to Kai Tak with you tomorrow, sir?'

'Certainly I'll take him. Give me a chance to practise my Cantonese. Tell him to be at the camp gate at 8 AM. Sharp, mind you.'

'Yes, sir. Sharp.'

Came 8 AM and the Unit Commander drove out of the camp gate in his jeep. A Chinese, clad in the white vest and khaki shorts that make his kind indistinguishable from one another, was standing by the gate, grinning.

'Don't stand there, grinning, you slab-sided, misbegotten offspring of a bolweevil,' said Lacey, practising his Cantonese.

The Chinese continued to grin, but made no move.

'Get in, blast you.' This time he beckoned.

The Cantonese, still smiling, even laughing slightly, came forward willingly. After a century of British occupation, the Hong Kongese have given up wondering about the strange inexplicable impulses of the red devils. He climbed into the seat next to Lacey and sat holding tightly to the windscreen frame while the jeep raced and bounded over the ten or fifteen miles to Kai Tak.

Lacey ushered him into Sick Quarters. 'Here you are, Doc: our new Officers' Mess cook. Give him the once-over, will you please.'

The Chinese, delighted and flattered by all the attention he was receiving, submitted willingly to the rather intimate tests to which he was subjected and the inoculations and vaccination which were pumped into his arm. His new employer left a message at the Civilian Labour Office in Station Headquarters to say that he was returning to his unit and cookie must make his own way: there was a good bus service.

As he drove into the gates of his GCI he noticed that there was another Chinese standing there, with apparent aimlessness; odd, how these chaps seemed to have all day to hang around . . .'

The Adjutant met him with a reproving expression.

'Sir, you forgot to take the new cook into Kai Tak.'

'No, I didn't. He was having his medical, last time I saw him; he must have cleared the Labour Office by now. He'll be here in time to cook dinner.'

'But, sir, you were five minutes early. When he turned up, you'd gone.'

'But there was a man waiting at the gate, so I took him along.'

'Sir, that was the chap who'd come to dig the new latrines for the airmen . . .'

The joy of it was that, once the wheels had been put in motion to employ Wun Fat Tit as a cook, it took three months to reverse them and get him ejected.

But Squadron Leader Lacey was there to do a job and he did it well. On 8th November 1951 the Air Officer Commanding Hong Kong, Air Commodore D. W. F. Bonham-Carter, CB, DFC, wrote to him:

Dear Lacey,
    The Hong Kong Auxiliary Air Force has communicated

to my Headquarters a message of gratitude for the exemplary co-operation they received from your Unit in the training of their radar operators during the Annual Camp.

Whilst the message refers to all personnel of No. 43 SU, it cites, in particular, Flight Lieutenant Grocott, Sergeant Locks and Corporal Harris.

I am aware of the long struggle which the formation and training of the FCU has involved, and it is most gratifying to me to receive confirmation of your Unit's efforts in this task.

Will you please convey this message to all operations personnel under your command.

Yours sincerely,

Two and a half years later, Lacey returned to England and was posted, as a flight lieutenant, to be a ground instructor at the Initial Training School, Jurby, Isle of Man. Thence the school moved to Kirton Lindsey, Lincolnshire. He did not enjoy the job, despite the compensation it offered of a great deal of gliding.

Badly out of flying practice, he applied to go on the Pilot Attack Instructors' Course at the Fighter Weapons School, Leconfield, Yorkshire. The CO, an old friend of his, told him that he would like to keep him on as an instructor if he did well enough on the course.

The PAI course is a difficult one at any time. To a man of thirty-six who has not held a full-time flying appointment for four years, it must have been a formidable strain. But he stayed on, at the end of the three months, to be a Flight Commander and Instructor.

He instructed at the Fighter Weapons School until March 1957, when he was sent to Germany to serve as a Fighter Controller once more. Typically, he formed a close friendship with Major Eric Hohagen, a Luftwaffe pilot whom he describes as someone who 'must have been an absolute joy to Hitler. Over six feet tall, fair and handsome; even though he had several accidents during the war, which have left marks on his face.' What Lacey admires most about Hohagen is that he served throughout the war in the yellow-nosed 'Goering Squadron' based at Abbeville; the toughest of all German fighter units. And that he never claims that any of his eighty confirmed victories were gained on the Russian front, but admits with pride that they were won against the British and the Americans. Major Hohagen, who was taken from hospital with his injuries only part-healed to fly the Me 263 jet fighter in 1944, now flies Sabrejets for the Luftwaffe.

The tour in Germany did more for Lacey's command of foreign languages than his 2½ years in Hong Kong had done. 'I acquired a certain amount of pub, restaurant and garage German. I could order a meal or a drink and get what I wanted, and tell the garage exactly what was wrong with the car. Of course my conversational German wasn't so good – unless it happened to be about drink, food or cars.'

Back to England, in September 1959, and a posting to a GCI once more, on fighter control duties; but this time, by choice, in his native Yorkshire where he has bought a house and, with his wife Sheila and three daughters Diana fourteen, Wendy eleven and Susie who was born in June 1960, lives happily among his friends, who are mainly fishermen.

Flamborough, he describes as 'A wonderful little place. It's well over a year now since I've had to buy any fish: in this village the fishermen push a fish in at your door as they pass in the early morning on their way home from sea. They'd never think of letting you know who dropped the fish in.'

And that is the story of Ginger Lacey. The pilot who learned to fly on Tiger Moths and progressed to Hunters, but who now has the opportunity only to fly Chipmunks and no longer bothers to enter his flying hours in his log-book. 'It doesn't seem worth while. There seems to be no purpose to flying when there are no longer any aircraft to shoot at or trains and tanks to fire on with your rockets.'

Tempus edax rerum.

Epilogue

'JIMMIE NUTTI'

No story that concerns No. 17 Squadron in the Second World War should omit mention of the squadron mascot, christened 'Jimmie Nutti' and more usually known as 'Chico'.

In 1942, the squadron was flying Hurricanes from Red Road air strip in Calcutta, and living in the suburb of Alipore three miles away.

Every day, starving native children used to gather outside the Messes, begging for food. The youngest of these, who was apparently in the care of a twelve-year-old girl, was a little Gurkha boy aged about three. Not only was he starving and homeless, but seriously ill with malaria.

Warrant Officer Bill Williams took charge of him and had him admitted to the British Military Hospital.

The squadron adopted him, added the prefix 'James' to his names of Nattu Alis Salim, and he became 'Jimmie Nutti', affectionately 'Chico' to everyone, officers and airmen.

Chico went everywhere with the squadron, was supported by a fund to which the members regularly contributed, and used to appear on pay parade with the troops.

When the squadron left Malaya to go to Japan, he was left in good hands at RAF Butterworth, with a substantial sum of money to give him a start in life.

Nothing was heard of him, and at a squadron reunion in 1960, fifteen years later, it was decided to try to trace him.

The help of the *Staits Times* was sought, and newspapers throughout Malaya carried the story of Jimmie Nutti. An immediate response came from an Indian schoolteacher in Singapore, who used to be Chico's schoolmate when the latter was taken daily between the RAF station at Butterworth (on the mainland opposite Penang Island) and St Mark's School.

Later, the Gurkha boy passed into the care of a clergyman, until the latter left for Borneo, when Jimmie Nutti was looked after by the Headmaster of the school.

In 1954, Chico left Butterworth for Singapore, where he joined the Merchant Service.

Late in 1960 the former member of 17 Squadron who was tracing him, established that he was putting himself through an engineering course, at Greer Technical Institute, Chicago, Illinois; and studying from 8 AM to 2 PM and working to earn money from 3.30 PM to 12.30 AM in order to do so.

Moreover, he had entered the USA illegally, and this had to be put right officially for him by the same former 17 Squadron pilot.

He has since then appeared in a 'This Is Your Life' programme in Hollywood, and been visited by one of the squadron's ex-members from Canada. Finally, he was found a good job to go to on completing his course and obtaining a Mechanic's Certificate.

FOR THE RECORD

3rd September 1939	Posted to No. 501 (County of Gloucester) Squadron as Sergeant Pilot.		
10th May 1940	Squadron posted to France.		
13th May 1940	Me 109 E ⎫ Same		Destroyed
13th May 1940	He 111 K ⎭ combat		Destroyed
13th May 1940	Me 110		Destroyed
	Awarded Croix de Guerre.		
27th May 1940	He 111 K ⎫ Same		Destroyed
27th May 1940	He 111 K ⎭ combat		Destroyed
	Mentioned in Dispatches.		
19th June 1940	Squadron returned from France.		
20th July 1940	Me 109 E		Destroyed
	Awarded Distinguished Flying Medal.		
12th August 1940	Ju 87 B ⎫ Same		Destroyed
12th August 1940	Ju 87 B ⎭ combat		Probable
15th August 1940	Do 17		Damaged
16th August 1940	Me 109 E		Probable
24th August 1940	Ju 88		Destroyed
24th August 1940	Do 215		Damaged
29th August 1940	Me 109 E		Destroyed
30th August 1940	Me 110 Jaguar		Probable
30th August 1940	He 111 K		Destroyed
31st August 1940	Me 109 E		Destroyed
2nd September 1940	Me 109 E		Destroyed
2nd September 1940	Do 215 ⎫ Same		Damaged
2nd September 1940	Me 109 E ⎭ combat		Destroyed
5th September 1940	Me 109 E ⎫ Same		Destroyed
5th September 1940	Me 109 E ⎭ combat		Destroyed
13th September 1940	He 111 K		Destroyed
15th September 1940	Me 109 E ⎫ Same		Destroyed
15th September 1940	Me 109 E ⎭ combat		Damaged

| 15th September 1940 | He 111 K ⎱ Same | Destroyed |
| 15th September 1940 | Me 109 E ⎰ combat | Destroyed |

Awarded Bar to DFM

27th September 1940	Me 109 E	Destroyed
30th September 1940	Ju 88	Damaged
7th October 1940	Me 109 E	Probable
12th October 1940	Me 109 E	Destroyed
26th October 1940	Me 109 E	Destroyed
30th October 1940	Me 109 E ⎱ Same	Destroyed
30th October 1940	Me 109 E ⎰ combat	Damaged
15th January 1941	Commissioned Acting Pilot Officer.	
22nd June 1941	Promoted Acting Flight Lieutenant.	
10th July 1941	Me 109 E	Destroyed
14th July 1941	Me 109 E	Damaged
24th July 1941	Me 109 E ⎱ Same	Destroyed
24th July 1941	Me 109 E ⎰ combat	Destroyed
17th July 1941	He 59	Destroyed
18th August 1941	Posted to No. 57 Operation Training Unit, Hawarden.	
10th March 1942	Posted to No. 602 (City of Glasgow) Squadron.	
24th March 1942	FW 190	Damaged
25th April 1942	FW 190 ⎱ Same	Damaged
25th April 1942	FW 190 ⎰ combat	Damaged
7th May 1942	Posted to HQ No. 81 Group.	
27th May 1942	Promoted to Acting Squadron Leader.	
28th September 1942	Posted to Aircraft and Armament Experimental Establishment, Boscombe Down.	
30th November 1942	Posted to No. 1 Special Attack Instructor's School.	
June-July 1943	Arrived in India. Posted to No. 20 Squadron.	
6th July 1943	Posted to No. 1572 Gunnery Flight.	
August 1944	Posted to HQ 3rd Tactical Air Force.	
6th November 1944	Posted to command No. 155 Squadron.	

23rd November 1944	Posted to command No. 17 Squadron.
19th February 1945	'Oscar' (Nakajima Ki 43)
	Destroyed

This officer is entitled to wear the following medals: Distinguished Flying Medal and Bar, 1939–45 Star with Battle of Britain Clasp, Air Efficiency Award and Clasp, Air Crew Europe Star with Atlantic Clasp, Burma Star, Defence Medal, War Medal, Coronation Medal.

BRITISH ILLUSTRATED
BATTLES SERIES

WATERLOO 6/-
JOHN NAYLOR

'No commanders were ever better served by their men, British, French and Prussian ... graphic descriptions present a moving story of courage, devotion and endurance.'
British Army Review

AGINCOURT 6/-
CHRISTOPHER HIBBERT

'A straightforward and absorbing account of this astounding battle and the campaign that so improbably led up to it.'
The Observer

BATTLES OF THE '45 6/-
KATHERINE TOMASSON and FRANCIS BUIST

The story of the fiercely fought engagements which took place between the royal army and the Jacobites, led by Prince Charles Edward. 'History as it should be written ... infinite research and highly entertaining.' *Books and Bookmen*

THE SPANISH ARMADA 5/-
MICHAEL LEWIS

'A brilliantly clear picture of the campaign.'
British Book News

TRAFALGAR 5/-
OLIVER WARNER

'A stirring picture of the battle in which Nelson died destroying Napoleon's power at sea.' *New York Times*

GREAT MYSTERIES OF THE AIR
RALPH BARKER 5/-

A colourful collection of fourteen of the great puzzles associated with flights, including the tragedy of the deaths of the Duke of Kent and Leslie Howard, and the mystery of Amelia Earhart.

'The historical detail and accuracy, combined with the author's understanding of aviation, makes it something of a reference book as well as a real-life "whodunnit".'
FLYING REVIEW

FULL CIRCLE
(The story of air fighting) 6/-
AIR VICE-MARSHAL J. E. (Johnnie) JOHNSON, CBE, DSO, DFC

A fascinating account of air fights from the string, canvas and wood aircraft, armed with rifles and pistols, of the 1914-18 war, to the multi-machine guns, cannon and rocket-firing fighters of the Korean war.

'A gripping account of how air fighting began.'
EVENING NEWS